EVERY MOM

EVERY MOMENT COUNTS

A Life of Mary Butterwick

Carmel Thomason

DARTON · LONGMAN + TODD

First published in 2011 by
Darton, Longman and Todd Ltd
1 Spencer Court
140 – 142 Wandsworth High Street
London SW18 4JJ

ISBN: 978-0-232-52837-4

A catalogue record for this book is available from the British Library

Phototypeset by Kerrypress Ltd, Luton, Bedfordshire
Printed and bound in Great Britain by CPI Antony Rowe, Chippenham

This book is dedicated to my grandparents:

Eleanor Thomason who prayed with me and rooted my faith

Thomas Thomason who showed me what it means to contribute to a community

Henry Lucas whose generosity of spirit helped me to appreciate the good in a world we don't always understand

Eileen Lucas whose fun nature and kindness taught me how to enjoy life and to love one another

—Your memories will live with me always.

CONTENTS

FOREWORD

This is the story about the difference that one person can make. Nowadays we tend to expect others to meet our needs rather than accept responsibility ourselves; everything is so complicated that we don't know where to start. But we are all dependent ultimately on the vision of a number of individuals who are motivated somehow to make change. Mary Butterwick, at first the most unlikely candidate, is one of them.

In 2009, the Butterwick Trust celebrated its first twenty-five years. Now all sorts of people are committed to its future. It is with delight that we welcome this book about Mary and her story. It's a story well worth telling.

I have often told the story of how all this started. For a while, I was the parish priest at St Peter's in Stockton-on-Tees. I was not entirely clear who Mary was when she rang to ask to see me, other than being a member of our congregation. All I knew was that sadly she had lost her husband, John. I can see her now sitting in my study explaining this wild idea of hers. The idea wasn't really wild because hospice work was already being pioneered by Cicely Saunders in Oxford. It was just that Mary seemed the most unlikely person, in the most unlikely context, to pursue it. That shows how little I knew about her and her determination. I think I probably fobbed her off by telling her to go away for six months hoping that she would forget all about it. Well, she did not forget all about it and probably returned to see me earlier than forecast with the news that she had been beavering away, visiting, listening and finding allies. I wish now that I could remember those early conversations in more detail and recollect the initial meetings. Certainly it all resulted in action. With extraordinary tenacity she eventually opened up the house in Hartburn Lane. Some of us wondered how long it would last. The rest, they say, is history.

Mary involved me at the start for two reasons. First, she wanted to do things carefully and properly: she is a woman of considerable patience. She wanted me to know what one of my parishioners was up to. She hoped for my approval and she certainly received my support. Second, she wanted to share her faith with me. From the very start Mary believed that her hopes would only be fulfilled if God was in it too. She was quite clear about that and quite clear that she would accept disappointment if that was God's call.

So the Butterwick Trust was born amidst (on her part) a lot of prayer, reflection, quiet, retreat – but also with much honesty and laughter. This had one great advantage. As far as I can remember Mary never bullied anyone into her plans. She did not necessarily believe that she was right. She listened hard to what others said. Slowly but surely the Butterwick Trust was born through love and trust. From such a small and vulnerable start who could have believed what the first twenty five years has achieved. Of course, it's not just Mary's story now. All sorts of people have come on board with all sorts of practical skills and professional knowledge. People's lives have been changed. Not just the lives of the patients but the lives of everyone involved.

THE RT. REVD. STEPHEN PEDLEY
September 2010

PREFACE

I don't know why God heals some people and not others. Why some people die young and others go hungry. Life has no easy answers and isn't always fair. There are things we can do nothing about, but so often our perceived helplessness means that we do nothing about those things that we can change.

Mary Butterwick is proof that one person, no matter what age or circumstances, can make a difference – can help to create a better world.

At the time when she started campaigning for better palliative care, Mary was a 54-year-old widow who worked part-time in a tea factory. She had no medical background and no influential friends, but she believed in the power of love, recognised the importance of our smallest actions and had strength to speak her mind and take action against injustice.

I first met Mary when I was asked to interview her while working as a feature writer for the *Evening Gazette* in Middlesbrough. Her story struck an instant chord with me because my grandmother died following a very short illness, aged 52, in the same month that Mary lost her husband, John. It happened at opposite ends of the country, but the lack of care in the hospitals during that bitter cold winter, and the hurt this caused, were exactly the same. Of course it was a shock to lose someone so close, almost without warning, but it was the careless words, the lack of dignity and respect for life that created even deeper wounds, so hard to heal. If we both had experienced this, I knew that there must be hundreds, if not thousands, of others who felt the same.

Many years later, my grandfather died in St Ann's Hospice in Manchester. The contrast in care, while it didn't make the loss any less, meant that we were able to spend his last days enjoying our time together. As a family we all felt loved and cared for in a time of vulnerability. A kind word or a smile costs nothing. Why do we sometimes find the simplest gifts so hard to give?

Mary's story shows how the smallest of our actions can make a difference for the better or worse. In her frustration and grief she questioned God, but she also trusted him. Mary is not a theologian. She lives by the simple command to love your neighbour as you love yourself. Her faith is a practical one – she does her part and trusts that God will do what she can't. After spending many weekends listening to Mary's recollections, visiting the hospice and speaking to her friends, I wrote this story. The events described are true but, on Mary's request, some names have been changed.

May her achievement inspire you to step out in faith and do what you can, to never stop dreaming for a better world and to live every moment with love in your heart.

CARMEL THOMASON
July 2010

ACKNOWLEDGEMENTS

During the writing of this book Mary has taught me so much about enjoying life. I'd like to thank her for allowing me to tell her inspirational story and also for the love and friendship she has shared with me. I'd like to thank her family too as it is never easy to read about your loved ones as characters in a story, however encouraging that story may be.

Thank you to Valerie Rayner for sharing her early memories of the Butterwick Trust, the Rt Revd Stephen Pedley and all the staff and volunteers at the hospice who have welcomed me and make it the warm and loving place that it is today. I'm indebted to Robert Nichols, for patiently listening to my ideas and giving me a comfortable place to stay while I was visiting Mary.

I'd like to thank Virginia Hearn for her invaluable advice and careful editing, but most of all for her constant encouragement and for believing in me. Thanks also to all the wonderful staff at Darton, Longman and Todd who have made this possible.

Finally, I could not have written this book without the constant support and encouragement of my family who now probably know this story better than I do.

Part 1

LEARNING TO LIVE

1

MOMENTS AND MEMORIES

Mary always says that we should treasure the moment, because the life you think you have can change in an instant. One minute you're merrily sauntering down one road then all of a sudden the path changes and you find yourself hurtling in another direction. That's how it's been in her life, anyway.

Looking back, it's not always easy to see exactly where choices were made or where a different path might have led. Mary just trusts that whatever moments go into making a memory, to shaping a life, happen for a reason. To ask why is a whole other story, and one we might never understand.

For Mary, the memories begin one moment in 1928, at Trafford Park, Manchester. Gas light was just beginning to become popular, but, for the Wood family, candles were still the preferred method of lighting. Nothing, however, could ever dim the memory of what Mary saw in the kitchen that evening.

It was always a busy home, Mary being the fourth child of five; she had three older sisters, Doris, Jane and Isobella, and a younger brother, Jack. Maybe it was Doris's hands on her, holding her back, stopping her getting through the door. It might have been someone else, but it didn't matter. There, laid on the kitchen table, the table where her family sat and ate together every day, was little Jack. Their father, James, was holding Jack's head while a strange man cut into his throat with a sharp knife which shone in the light of the open fire.

Mary's tummy felt tight. She wanted to scream but no sound came. She felt she might be sick, but she wasn't. Dragged away from the scene, Mary ran to her room and shut the door. What was that man doing to Jack, and why wasn't Daddy stopping him? She buried her head in the blankets. They were making her face itchy but she didn't care, she just wanted the world to go away or, at least, the part of the world she had just experienced. If she couldn't see it then it didn't exist.

'Mary?' It was her father. 'Mary, how are you, Sugar Bun?'

Mary turned over to reveal a tear-streaked face.

'Hey, come here, it's okay. Jack is fine; everything is going to be all right.'

'Who was that man and why was he hurting Jack?' she cried.

'That was the doctor. Jack has been very poorly and the doctor had to cut his throat so that he could breathe properly. He's okay now, but he's still poorly so I don't want you crying and upsetting him, do you hear? You have to be a good strong girl for Mummy and Daddy.'

Mary threw her arms around her father and buried her head in his chest as the sobs came. He held her for a moment, then, with outstretched arms, looked her straight in the eye.

'Let me see that face. Now, what did I say about crying?'

Mary smiled shyly.

'That's better. Now, I don't want to see any more tears. You're the tough one in this family. I can't have you crying or else who will look after your brother?'

He blew out the candle beside her bed. Mary closed her eyes tightly and wished the hard pain in her chest would go away.

The next time Mary saw her brother it was through a doorway again. She could just about see his face if she got her gaze in the right place, standing on tip-toes to peer between starched white wimples of nuns, whose bowed heads nodded slowly as they prayed in hushed tones around the bed where Jack lay.

Jack made funny whistling noises as he breathed. He did that a lot. Her mother called it wheezing. She said that Jack made those noises because he had asthma, which meant that he couldn't breathe the same as everyone else. This time it was even more serious. The doctor said that Jack had pneumonia and might die. Well, they said that he probably would die, but Mary's parents didn't want to believe that. Neither of them were Catholics and she never knew where the nuns came from, but a small group regularly came to the house, dressed in black habits which trailed the floor, their faces small circles peeking out from what seemed to Mary like big triangular hats.

She watched as they knelt around Jack's bed and prayed for him to get better. She desperately hoped that he would too, if only so that her mother would have time to cuddle her as well.

The emergency tracheotomy saved Jack's life, but he remained a sickly child. The doctors said that he might outgrow his asthma after the age of seven, although none of them expected him to live that long. Proving them all wrong, he did live, and, proving them right at the same time, he also outgrew his asthma, but the pneumonia left him with only one healthy lung.

Once he was well enough to leave his bed his muscles had wasted so much that they were too weak to hold him and he was unable to walk. For weeks afterwards he would grab on to the fur of the family dog, Mona, a gentle collie, who would allow Jack to use her as a balance. Jack would pull himself up by the dog's coat and lean against her, as they made tentative steps together across the floor. Mary had always been told not to pull Mona's hair, but when Jack did it the dog didn't seem to mind; it was as if they understood each other – he never pulled too hard and Mona never let him fall.

One day their father took Mona for a walk and she never came back. Mary watched them go from the bedroom window. There was some story about her going to care for another little boy who needed her, but Mary never really believed it. Not that she questioned it. Mary learned early not to ask questions. 'Children should be seen and not heard,' she was told.

It wasn't as though the adults were doing much talking for them. No one spoke very much at all, certainly not about feelings. There was never any time. If her mother wasn't nursing Jack, she was scrubbing floors, washing, cooking or whatever else needed to be done, and there was always something that needed to be done.

There was one question, however, that Mary had to ask. She hadn't been able to settle since she heard Isobella scream down the stairs: 'Well, you're not my mother, so why should I do what you tell me?' Her mother shouted back and Isobella, only three years older but seeming much more grown up in Mary's eyes, screamed all the more

until Mary ran out of the house and hid at the bottom of the garden –
her favourite spot, next to the brightly coloured dahlias. Her father
loved those flowers and she loved sitting with him as he tended to
them. Her favourite part was watching earwigs climb the long
wooden sticks which had been placed in the plant pots to keep them
straight. It was fascinating to see their shiny clawed bodies crawl all
the way to the top, just to go back down again. She'd have secret bets
with herself as to which one would reach the top first. Here she could
forget all her worries; well, almost.

What Isobella had shouted was one worry that the earwigs
couldn't make disappear. Lifting herself up, Mary made her way back
into the house. It was quieter now. The shouting had stopped.
Isobella was nowhere to be seen and her mother was in the kitchen.
Mary looked at her from the door. She looked the same as she'd
always looked, wearing a long dress covered by a pinny and laced-up
boots, so long that they disappeared underneath the dress.

'Mummy?' Mary tugged at the pinny to make sure she knew this
was important.

'What is it?' Her mother turned with her hands full of flour.

'If you're not her mummy, are you not mine either?'

2

SO THIS IS LIFE

Mary's entrance into the world was not without its drama, but not for the reasons she first feared.

'This one is of no use,' the midwife declared, throwing her limp body under the bed.

It was 2 June 1924, exactly one year to the day that her parents, James Wood and Hilda John, married.

'Where's my baby? What have you done with my baby?' Hilda cried.

'She's dead, girl,' Hilda could smell the stench of alcohol on the midwife's breath.

'No!' Hilda screamed. 'Can't you do something? Please?'

'Well, I'll be off, love. Nothing more to be done here. You rest up.'

James came in to find his wife weeping, with a cry so deep it was as if her very soul was leaving her.

'Where's the baby?'

Her words barely audible, Hilda told him: 'She's dead.'

'But where is she?' he insisted. 'Hilda, where's our baby?'

Crawling under the bed, James reached out to his child, blue and lifeless with the umbilical cord wrapped around her neck. Lifting her up, he untied the cord and held her close. 'Hilda, there's some life in this one yet.'

Young Mary gasped for air and let out a cry. So this was life.

James and Hilda later learned that the midwife was struck off for being drunk on duty. Who knows how many other parents had been through the same ordeal, and how many had not been as fortunate to rescue their child before it was too late?

James took naturally to fatherhood. He'd had a lot of practice, bringing up his three daughters single-handedly after his first wife

died. However, his kind, gentle temperament was somewhat overlooked by Hilda's father, Joseph, who only saw a widower, 15 years
his daughter's senior.

It wasn't that Joseph was uncharitable. He had for many years
brought his two daughters up with only the help of a housekeeper,
after the untimely death of his own wife at 35. One moment she was
combing her hair, beautiful as ever in front of the mirror, the next she
gave out a cry and Joseph watched in disbelief as she fell to the floor.
He didn't know it then, but his wife had suffered a massive heart
attack. There was no rousing her and he knew instantly that she had
left him.

Joseph wanted what he believed was the best for his girls, but no
matter how much he tried to put his foot down and influence their
decisions, they always did what they wanted anyway. The eldest,
Edith, eloped, escaping through the bedroom window with Hilda's
help. It therefore only made matters worse when Hilda herself chose
to marry against his wishes, and, in his anger and disappointment, he
ended up disowning them both. Compared to others who shared his
start in life, Joseph was a wealthy man. An orphan, he had joined the
army as soon as he was old enough, and there he educated himself by
reading as many books as he could get his hands on, working his way
up the ranks to become a chief engineer on the Firth of Forth bridge.
On leaving the forces he had become a director of a steel works,
buying a house in Southport as well as owning one of the only motor
cars in the area.

Due to the family rift, Mary was five before she met her grandfather. Following Jack's illness, doctors advised James and Hilda that it
would be better for their son's health if he were to move out of the
city. Southport seemed the perfect option – not too far away, and it
was believed that the fresh sea air might do him good. Mending the
rift with her father after all these years was not going to be easy, but
Hilda was now determined to make amends.

Leaving the rest of the family at home, she and Mary boarded a
train at Manchester. Hilda wanted to make a good impression, to
show her father that, although he might not have agreed with her

choice of husband, things were working out well. Mary was to be proof of this, and Hilda made sure her daughter was dressed immaculately for the occasion.

Mary didn't understand the significance of the journey, but she found it exciting nonetheless, sitting with her back to the engine, looking down the never-ending railway line at what appeared to her like a jungle of weeds. Her mother had bought her a new dress, coat and gloves. Wearing them made Mary feel special. She was thrilled with her new outfit, but particularly the gloves, which were leather with a fur trim round the cuff – she was to keep them all her life, a beautiful reminder of that time she spent with her mother, just the two of them.

Grandfather Joseph had a huge moustache, which seemed to grow all the way to his ears and tickled Mary's face when she kissed him. He had strange hands too; he'd lost a thumb and a couple of fingers in an accident at work, but Mary didn't understand why they looked different. When Joseph noticed her looking he played a missing finger game with her, which made her laugh. Mary's father had played this same game with her, but never as well as this.

By everyone's account the meeting went well and the family moved to Southport, where Mary started school and enjoyed the freedom of riding her first bike. Life was good; for a while, anyway. That was until her father lost his job.

James was a welder by trade and when the great depression caused a collapse in the demand for ships his work in the shipyards went with it. Hilda began to take in laundry to try to eke out a living, but for James there was no work to be found.

It was hard, but the family by no means bore the worst of the 1930s slump years. Even as a child, Mary knew that. She still had shoes, while most of her friends made do with wooden clogs and many more children and adults walked barefoot.

Joseph's money saved them from the harshest conditions. When the depression hit, he gave Hilda enough money to buy a shop, which she also ran as a small café, serving up steaming bowls of Lancashire hot pot.

However, while it saved them financially, the strain on the family was evident.

'I thought you were going to help me in the shop today?' Hilda asked James, not for the first time.

'What was that?' he mumbled, without looking up from his newspaper.

'Are you deaf or something?'

'I didn't hear you ask me to help you today.'

'Did you not hear or did you conveniently forget?'

'I don't know what I'd do there anyway,' he said, wearily. 'I've been looking for work all day and I'm tired. I'm going in the garden.'

James never did help out in the shop. He did, however, keep looking for work in the shipyards, and eventually found some at Haverton Hill Shipyard in Teesside.

By this time his eldest daughers, Doris and Jane, were working in Lyons Corner tea house, so the three sisters stayed on in Southport while James, originally a Jarrow man, moved the rest of his family to the North East.

Although the shop had to go, Hilda did get some say in the move. Arriving, in a furniture lorry, at an address James had organised for them, she promptly told the removal men: 'Don't you dare unload, we are not stopping here.'

They didn't, and Hilda managed to find them a more suitable home in Vicarage Street. Shortly after, the family moved again to Vicarage Avenue, Newtown, in Stockton-on-Tees, where Mary joined the junior school. She later moved to Newham Grange for her secondary education, before transferring to Stockton technical college, where she signed up for a business studies course learning bookkeeping, her parent's choice.

Then war broke out and the family was uprooted again.

3

A TEENAGER'S WAR

The air raid sirens, although always startling, had become a familiar sound to Mary.

The noise – shrill tones so loud they blocked out any thought – had become almost a nightly routine. Yet each time the sirens induced fresh panic, and, with adrenaline racing through her veins, Mary would grab what she could and run for shelter, praying that she would still have a home and, indeed, a life when the all clear sounded.

This night wasn't as bad as some of the others. At least the family had finished eating – Mary hated having to leave any food on her plate, especially when it was rationed to begin with. She also hated sleeping on the hard mattress under the stairs, but it was the safest place and, as uncomfortable as it was, she knew if she woke up the next morning with the house still standing that she had been one of the lucky ones.

'This is no good,' her father said, opening the cupboard door to let in the light of the morning.

'Let's just thank the Lord we are still here,' Hilda responded, gently stroking Jack's hair as he slept as soundly as if it were a luxury chamber. He must have exhausted himself from coughing, Mary thought, watching the dust dance on the daylight before following her parents out into the hall.

Her father was serious: 'Of course I'm thankful, but that's not what I mean. I don't want this for us, for you, every night – this danger, worrying whether we'll all be here or not in the morning.'

'We're at war, dear,' Hilda said gently. 'I don't think there's much we can do about it.'

'Yes, there is,' he sounded determined. 'I've been thinking about it and I've decided: you should all go back to Southport.'

Mary wanted to ask: 'Why?' Last night's raid hadn't seemed any worse than any other. She didn't ask though; her mother was asking enough questions for both of them and, whatever the reason, her father was resolute.

At 16, it was hard for Mary to value the enormity of war as her parents did; it had crept up on her without any real knowledge of how or why it had begun. Still, she was aware that this wasn't just a battle for the soldiers. This war affected everyone and, while no one could ever be said to have gotten used to it, Mary, like most people at the time, adapted to its hardships.

Back in Southport, she took her first job in the office of an ammunitions factory and escaped, when she could afford it, in the love stories of the silver screen. Her pay packet was half a crown (2/6p), from which she budgeted for silk stockings and her bus fares to work. However, most days Mary chose to walk to work, saving her pennies for a visit to the picture house.

Going to the cinema on the High Street was a real treat. Mary loved the whole ritual of it – being shown to her seat by flashlight, ordering a tray of tea and having it placed on her knee with a plate of biscuits, before settling down to enjoy the Hollywood romances played out by her favourite studio icons, Ginger Rogers and Fred Astaire, or Nelson Eddy and Jeanette MacDonald. It cost two shillings, almost all the pocket money from her wages, but for Mary it was worth it – the experience made her feel a million dollars.

Meanwhile, back on Teesside, James was starting to question the wisdom behind the idea of his family living in a coastal safe-haven while he continued to work in the shipyards. The reality of his daily life – returning home to an empty house, cooking (something he'd never had to do and decided he didn't enjoy at all – neither the making nor the eating of what he rustled up), sheltering during air raids and waking up alone just to do it all over again – was starting to get him down.

Catching himself in the mirror one day, he thought: 'What am I doing? I even look a mess without Hilda to look after me.'

Their street was next in line to be allocated Anderson shelters for the bottom of the gardens. It wouldn't stop the bombings of course, but at least it would be safer than hiding under the stairs or the kitchen table.

'Yes – once the Anderson shelter is built I'll bring them back,' he told himself. 'I can't stand being apart any longer. At least this way, if we go, we all go together.'

And so they returned to Newtown. The new outdoor shelters were believed to be much safer than the protection of a staircase or cellar, although this fact didn't stop Mary's heart from pounding at the roar of planes overhead or the screeching of bombs being dropped, leaving her waiting for the implosion, praying that the family would live to see daylight. Still, as precarious as life was, it had to go on, and Mary quickly found a new job working in the office of wholesale grocers Jarman & Flint in Stockton, where she learned far more than professional typing.

'Ok, Mary, break time! You come with me,' Enid ordered, and Mary promptly followed. Well, Enid was in charge after all, but even if she hadn't been Mary didn't think her the sort of woman you'd argue with.

While the tea was brewing, Enid opened her packet of cigarettes and offered it to Mary.

'Sorry, I don't smoke,' she refused, politely.

Enid began to laugh. 'You what?'

'I don't smoke.'

Enid snorted: 'We've a right one here. Well you'll best learn hadn't you, because you can't call yourself a lady unless you can smoke.'

She handed Mary a cigarette, who took one puff and almost retched coughing, which only made Enid laugh all the more.

'All right, back to work,' she ordered. Winking at Mary, she added: 'Don't worry, we'll keep practising until you get it right.'

It wasn't too long before Mary was inhaling properly. Of course, at that time no one knew about the health risks associated with smoking. It was the fashionable thing to do. Smoking was part of being a grown-up and you were not considered to be smoking unless you inhaled.

It was turning out to be a good day, which only got better when a Third Battalion Grenadier Guard walked through the door, grabbing everyone's attention, not least Mary's. She had never seen such a soldier before. He was tall, something she always noticed first – being 6 feet tall herself, it was rare to see a man who was taller than her – and stood as straight as a ramrod.

Most unexpectedly, Mary found herself accepting a date – her first real date – all the more exciting because it was with a real soldier, Frank the Grenadier Guard. The date led to her first kiss, which, she might add, was very romantic and certainly never forgotten. Now she really was a grown up.

Being a grown-up also meant making some of one's own decisions, but, as Mary was still living under her parents' roof, that wasn't always easy. Her cousin, Peggy, was two years older and it seemed to her mother that whatever was good for Peggy was good for Mary too.

'Peggy is going to secretarial college,' Hilda said over supper, with an intonation that made Mary aware her mother was stating more than fact in her remark. 'I think that would be ideal for you, Mary.'

Next, it was: 'Peggy's got a lovely little office job, Mary. I think it would be just the kind of thing that would suit you.'

Then: 'I've heard there is an office job going at Jarman & Flint. It sounds just perfect. I think we should pay them a visit.'

Indeed it was a perfect job – for someone who enjoyed office work. Mary loved Peggy, but she didn't love office work. Nevertheless, she didn't feel that she could voice her opinion because it would have been so strongly against her parents' wishes. The novelty of the job and all the characters who came with it kept her interested initially, but after a while Mary found sitting at a typewriter boring and she quickly became restless. 'There is a war on – surely I can be doing something more useful than this?' she thought.

Wasting no time, she signed up to join the land army that afternoon. She was beaming with delight and couldn't wait to rush home to tell her parents what she'd done. Then, running down the road, she heard a sound that made her heart sink. The quickest route home meant walking past the slaughterhouse. Usually, apart from the smell of course, it was fine. This time, however, she could hear the noise of the cows being walked in to their death, and Mary would rather take the long route home, which was a mile out of her way, than pass them.

'Your tea is cold, Mary. Where have you been?' Hilda asked, believing that her daughter had not been up to any mischief other than avoiding the cows.

'You know I can't walk past that slaughterhouse when the cows are going in, Mother.'

'You eat them, don't you? How do you think the meat gets on your plate?'

Mary didn't answer. In fact she felt slightly guilty because it wasn't out of sympathy for those poor cows that she couldn't walk past them. When it came down to it, she just didn't like cows, or, rather, she was scared of them with their huge, bulging bodies and flared nostrils. Not to mention the noise from the slaughterhouse – the moos were frantic and deafening! It was almost as if the beasts were screaming. Well, she supposed, you would, wouldn't you, if you were being led to your death? That's if they knew, of course, and whatever anyone said, she had a hunch that they did. Anyway, she didn't want to think about that now, she had much more important news: 'I'm joining the land army!'

4

BLASTED COWS

The prospect of being freed from her desk and let loose in the countryside was like a dream come true. Mary was to go to Penrith in Cumbria to do three months training, and she couldn't wait. As with so many dreams, however, the reality didn't quite match up.

'I can't believe it,' she thought. 'Not cows. Please don't say I've got to milk those cows?'

'For God's sake girl, what are you doing?' shouted one of the farmhands. It was the first morning and she knew hardly anyone, but it seemed that didn't stop strangers from yelling at you.

Mary stood still, trying to get her breath, before she could speak.

The man shouted again: 'You look like a raving lunatic running after those cows!'

'Well, I've been told to bring them for milking. How else am I supposed to get them to move? You tell me,' she huffed defensively.

The farmhand smiled; she was a feisty one. 'These cows do this every day – they know where they're going,' he said, his voice softer now.

'Well, how was I supposed to know that?' she said, embarrassed.

'Well, I guess you do now, city girl,' he laughed. 'If you relax, the cows will saunter up in their own good time.'

Mary smiled nervously. Relax – how could she do that when the milking was still to come?

After the three months training was up, all the trainees were called into a room to find out where they were to be billeted.

'Mary Wood – you will be going to Newmarket, where you will be placed in charge of a herd of cows.'

Her heart sank as she replied: 'Yes, sir.' Taking in the news, she closed her eyes briefly, wondering: 'What on earth am I going to do now?'

Arriving at her post at a farm on the outskirts of Newmarket, Suffolk, she couldn't believe the amount of land around her. The landlord, Mr Robertson, must be one hell of a wealthy man, she thought. He lived in what looked to Mary like a huge mansion on top of the hill and owned every bit of land around it, as far as the eye could see. Of course, Mary didn't get to stay in the gentleman's grand dwelling. There were several smaller cottages on the land for the farmhands and Mary was shown to one of those, where she would live with the wife of a cattleman, who had joined the army, and their two children.

At home Mary had by no means been used to luxury, but this cottage was basic even by the standards of the day. There were none of the facilities to which she had become accustomed. Her bed was a piece of canvas on the landing, but hey – she was in the countryside doing her bit and nothing, not even an uncomfortable night's sleep, was going to dull her excitement. Or so she thought.

'What the heck?' The sound of cows outside the window had made her wake with a start. She looked at the clock: five o'clock in the morning. 'So I guess that's my alarm clock,' she thought, 'they are not going to shut up until I milk them.' Pulling on her breeches, she got to work without so much as a wash or a drink.

'I bet he's done this on purpose,' Mary thought, cursing Mr Robertson as she milked each cow in turn to relieve them, and, in doing so, stopping the deafening moos. 'He will have known they'd be outside this house – that's why he's put me in here, I'm sure of it.'

After milking, Mary tidied herself up and ate a welcome breakfast; she was ravenous and everything tasted so good here. She especially savoured the fresh milk from the cow – richer and creamer than any she had tasted before – and thought that perhaps the advantages would outweigh the troubles of milking.

After breakfast there was still a lot to be done, but it was a lovely sunny morning and, as she made her way down the path, breathing the earthy smell of the farm deep into her lungs, Mary felt sure that her new boss was bound to be pleased at how quickly she'd responded to the herd – she would be the best land girl he ever knew.

'Mary!' It was him.

'Yes, Mr Robertson, sir?'

'Where are those blasted cows?' he shouted.

Mary stared into the empty field. 'I don't know,' she answered nervously. Where could they have got to in such a short time?

'So, you can't find them?' he said, sarcastically, his voice still raised slightly.

Mary looked around frantically. 'No, I can't find them,' she panicked.

'No, you can't,' he said dismissively. 'Do you know why?'

'No, sir,' she replied, sheepishly.

'Because they are all over the blasted estate, that's why!' he was shouting now. Someone had left the gate open and the cows had wandered out. Mary hadn't been anywhere near the gate and, apart from milking, she hadn't done anything to upset his precious cows. Of course she still got the blame – so much for impressing him with her early start.

Making her way to the stables, head down and despondent, Mary heard a woman's voice: 'Hey, young 'un. Don't you be worrying yourself about him.'

Mary turned. It was a woman from the estate who looked about her mother's age. She wore a pretty headscarf tied around the front and her cheeks were ruddy from spending so much time outdoors.

'Oh, I'm ok, I'll be fine, thank you,' Mary chirped.

'Here,' she beckoned her over. 'What's your name?'

'Mary. Mary Wood.'

'Well, Mary Wood, you've only been here a day and already you're getting his goat, eh?'

Mary looked embarrassed, 'I didn't do anything, it's just he thought …'

'You don't have to convince me of your innocence, dear,' she interrupted. 'I doubt it will have been any of your doing. I feel desperately sorry for any land girl on this farm.'

'Why do you say that?' Mary asked.

'Oh, I know the man. Anyway, look at the state of you. You look like you could do with a good scrub. Come to my house if you like – I've got a place you can get cleaned up.'

'Why, that's very kind of you …'

'The name's Mrs Scholes. You can call me Ann,' she offered.

'Thank you, Mrs Scholes – I mean, Ann – I would like to do that.' Mary was genuinely pleased, as there were no proper washing facilities in the cottage and she did feel rather grubby, but she was keener to know more about the master of the house. 'But first, what do you mean by you know the man?' she asked.

'Oh, he's got more money than he knows what to do with, that one.'

'So?' Mary was genuinely confused. 'That's no reason to feel sorry for me.'

'Did you not hear the story?' she whispered.

'What story?'

'Oh, I'm not sure I should tell you,' Ann was playing hard to get, but Mary guessed that really she was loving it and couldn't wait to spill gossip to the new face in the village.

'That sounds a bit ominous; you can't just say something like that and then leave.'

Ann needed little persuasion: 'Okay then, I suppose you'll find out for yourself sooner or later.' She looked around conspiratorially. 'The previous land girl – shot off his land she was, by his nibs himself.'

'No!' Mary was shocked.

'Indeed it's true. Rumour is she was having an affair with one of the farmhands. When old misery guts found out, he came down with a shotgun one morning and threatened her. Said if she didn't get off his land that instant, he'd shoot her off it.'

'What?' Mary was open-mouthed.

'Yeah, so, you'd better behave or he might use that gun for real next time. A nutter he is, that man, I'm telling you. Be warned – he's a real nutter.'

Mary had no intention of misbehaving. In fact, she hadn't done anything wrong to warrant being shouted at in the first place and certainly had no intention of messing about with any farmhands. She was still writing to her Grenadier Guard, Frank, although she scarcely heard from him now he was back on the frontline and when she did the army censors had blanked out such huge sections of his letters that they were barely readable.

As the days went by, Mary began to love her work on the farm. She didn't enjoy the stories she was hearing about her boss, but nevertheless, the work, although heavy, was invigorating. She smiled to herself; life was good – she was even getting to like the cows.

Life on the farm became a natural routine. Waking up to the cows' noisy call was something she'd probably never get used to, but once up she was ready for the day. The first task of the morning was to set the electrical milking machines going, and then finish the job by hand; that was called 'stripping the cows', she learned.

Sitting on her little milkmaid's stool one morning, Mary's thoughts drifted for a second before, suddenly, the next cow lifted its back leg up and knocked her flying off her stool. Without thinking, Mary put her hand out to save herself from falling but the cow stood right on it.

'Aarrghhhh, get off, you big lump!' she screamed. She was pinned down firm, the cow so heavy that she couldn't even reach around with her other hand to give it a nudge. 'Help!'

The next thing she knew, the farmer was standing over her, pouring a full bottle of iodine into the wound.

'Aarrghhhh!' she screamed again.

'You're back with us now then,' he laughed. 'Ellen heard you screaming, but when I found you, you were flat out, not saying a word. Best way, I say.'

Mary could see the bone sticking through the back of her hand, and, trying to hold back the screams, began to make muffled yelping noises as Mr Robertson wrapped the bandage. Although slightly rough, he handled her wound with an expert touch which Mary found comforting; obviously he'd dressed similar injuries a million times before, she thought.

'Okay, you'll be fine now.' He stood up from the running board where they'd been seated.

'Thank you,' Mary whimpered, looking down at her new fabric fist with sad eyes.

'So, what are you waiting for?'

Mary looked at him. He was serious.

'There are pigs to be fed yet – get back to work!'

If she could walk she could work, and she didn't get so much as a cup of tea until her rightful break time.

Mary worked from the sun coming up until the sun going down. If she wasn't looking after animals, she was clearing out stables or haymaking. There was always something to be done, but because she loved being outdoors she found it no hardship.

Then, about a year after first arriving at the farm, Mary became unwell, and this time no amount of clever bandaging could get her back into the fields.

'Where's Mary? Can't she hear those blasted cows?' Mr Robertson yelled, his voice bellowing all the way up the stairs and into the bedroom where Mary lay.

'She's very sick, Mr Robertson,' Mrs Knowles, the herdsman's wife whose cottage she was sharing, explained.

'She'll have been eating my darn plums, I bet. I'll give her today and, if she's not back on that land tomorrow, I'll be in that bedroom to ask why!'

Mary heard the door slam behind him.

'Mary, are you awake, love?' It was Mrs Knowles.

'I've never been near his plums, Mrs Knowles, honestly I haven't.'

'It's okay, my dear,' she comforted. 'Here, try this and see how you go.' She handed Mary a small glass of warm milk. 'This might settle your stomach.'

It didn't. Mary couldn't hold anything down and began to get weaker. After his initial outburst, even Mr Robertson became concerned about her condition. It wasn't like Mary to skive off her duties, he knew that. Maybe she had eaten something she shouldn't have, but, whatever it was, he wasn't going to be forking out for a doctor to find out. There was no place for illness on his farm. The only thing he could do was to send for the girl's mother – she could look after her.

It was a difficult journey home on the train, but, once back in her mother's care, Mary's strength began to grow.

'Your daughter, Mrs Wood, has a serious bout of gastroenteritis, and under no circumstances must go back to the farm.' The doctor tried to cut Mary from the conversation, but her young ears picked up everything.

Not realising that Mary had heard it all, Hilda waited a few days before breaking the news. She thought that the long train journey, coupled with the wait for a doctor, had been enough to cope with. Mary, however, stuck to the belief that once her strength had built back up she would return to her work. But, once she was properly up and about again, Hilda handed her a piece of paper which shattered her dreams.

'What's this, Mother?'

'Read it and see.'

'What? I can't believe it! Why? Why would you do that?' Mary was distraught. The paper was her discharge out of the land army. Her mother must have sent off the doctor's note to the authorities, who had discharged her as unfit.

'But I'm fine now, Mother,' she cried. 'I was there for a whole year and never got ill until now. I'm the strong one, remember. Let me go back, please!'

Hilda looked at her daughter; her sadness pained her too, but she couldn't let her go back to that farm, especially not after she'd seen the man she'd been slaving away for all this time.

'Mr Jarman is coming round this morning, so you'd better wipe those tears and clean yourself up,' she told her.

'But I don't want to go back to Jarman & Flints, Mother. You know I hate it there.'

'I've had a word with Mr Jarman and he's offering you a promotion in the office, with double the wages you were on before.'

Mary was silent. 'It's a good offer, Mary. You'll do well to take it.'

Mary accepted the offer for her parents' sake, but it didn't mean that she had changed her view on office work. Once back behind a desk, she pined for the wind in her hair and the mud on her boots. She even missed those blasted cows, as Mr Robertson always referred to them.

For Mary, office work was a chore and she never took kindly to doing anything she didn't want to do. She stuck it out for three months until, one lunch time, she could stand it no more. She hopped on a bus to Middlesbrough, walked into the recruitment office and joined the army.

Feeling both excited and proud, she announced her news back home, blurting it out as soon as she got through the door.

'Well, I'm in the army now,' she beamed.

'In the what?' obviously her mother didn't share her enthusiasm.

'In the army.'

'I heard what you said. I just can't believe it!' Hilda was exasperated, after she'd sorted such a good job for her at the office as well.

'Well, I am,' Mary insisted. 'I'll be getting a letter soon, saying where I've got to report to.'

There was going to be trouble, but for once Mary really didn't care.

5

BOMBS AND BUDDIES

Mary's army days began with three months training at Fenham Barracks in Newcastle, after which time she was given the choice of being either a driver or an ack-ack (an anti-aircraft gun operator). However, for Mary there was no real choice. Although she was more than ready to do her bit for the war effort, when it came to it, the thought of using a large gun to shoot down enemy aeroplanes was … well, it was simply unthinkable.

'An ack-ack!' she thought, having to stop the words bursting from her mouth as the realisation hit her. 'That's those guns, isn't it? I can't do that!'

Learning to drive in Camberley became the only option, but it was by no means an easy one. Joining a group of about half a dozen drivers, she found herself in charge of an open coal truck for a 20-minute lesson, before jumping in the back and holding on for dear life while the others took their turns at the wheel. The secrecy required of war conditions meant that there were no road signs to follow and no street lights during black out, leaving them to rely on a single slit in one of the headlights to guide the way.

At the end of each day Mary thought it a miracle that any of the group had survived. Yet, by the time the three months were up, she had begun to enjoy it and was driving anything she was given keys to, including heavy goods wagons, without a second thought.

Her first posting was north again, attached to the Royal Army Service Corps based at a large house in Perth, Scotland, which was to become her home for the following six-and-a-half years.

Mary loved the house, but, even more than that, she loved the five women she shared it with – Enid from Elgin, Kath from Wick,

Audrey from Rotherham, Beth from Redcar and Marion from Orkney – the 'Billiard Room Gang', so named because that was the room allocated as their dorm.

It was a grand space, lined with original solid wood panelling. In the centre was an open coke stove, where the girls would huddle together to keep warm. The Scottish winters were bitter, even for a northern lass. At these times the floor-to-ceiling French windows, which provided such a lovely view of the gardens in the summer, failed to let in an inch of daylight as heavy snowfall drifted against them. The two-blanket allowance simply wasn't enough, and most nights the girls would sneak in extra fuel to keep the coke stove burning secretly. At nine o'clock, when the non-commissioned officer on duty, or the NCO as the girls referred to her, shouted: 'Right, lights out girls!', that was when the real fun started. As soon as the NCO disappeared, one of the gang would switch on the light and another would be jumping out of the window, coke bucket in hand, to fill from a heap they'd found stashed at the back of the house.

Another way of keeping warm, they discovered, was to sneak into the kitchen after dark and fill lemonade bottles with boiling water. Many times this backfired when a bottle burst in the bed and, to cover their tracks, the girls had the double problem of sneaking out the glass and drying the bed.

For Mary, the mischief and camaraderie was all part of the excitement of being away from home. 'I'd die for these girls,' she smiled to herself, remembering one of the numerous times when her loyalty was put to the test. The girls were attached to the Royal Army Corps and there were so many men that every night it seemed one or other of the gang would have a date with a different Highlander. However, little did the suitor know that a date with one of the girls meant the others were close behind in the shadows.

'Come on, rubber legs,' Kath pulled affectionately at Mary's arm. 'They've gone outside, let's go.'

Mary quickly downed her half of black and tan, her then favourite mix of lager and stout, even though she knew it would go straight to her legs, hence the nickname. She wasn't in the habit of wasting anything, especially not a drink that had been paid for.

'Ooops,' Mary giggled, losing her footing slightly and falling onto Kath as the night air hit her.

'Shush, he'll hear you!'

The pair tip-toed to join the others crouching in the bushes, within sight but not quite ear-shot, of Enid and her date.

'What's he say?' Mary whispered.

'Shush,' Beth warned. 'If you kept quiet we might be able to hear.'

Mary and Kath rolled their eyes. It was no fun if you couldn't hear what was being said. A compliment was always so much better shared. Just as they were squabbling among themselves about what might or not might not be being said, Enid's voice came loud and clear: 'No, don't. Please?'

The soldier had flung his arms around her and was trying to pin her against a wall. 'Get off her!' Mary screamed, jumping out of the bushes and onto his back. The soldier shrugged her off, pushing both girls to the ground. Turning to face another four angry females, he decided against any further fight, spat on the ground dramatically and left.

'Well, I …' Kath started.

'Leave it,' said Beth sensibly. 'Let's go.'

Enid was a little shaken, but it was nothing that a late night giggle with her friends couldn't cure.

'Mary got a letter from her sailor today,' Audrey teased.

'He is not my sailor,' Mary insisted.

'Well, why does he keep writing to you?' Marion smiled.

'I don't blooming well know, do I?'

'So, let's find out,' Audrey giggled, dangling the letter provocatively in front of Mary's face.

'Give me that,' Mary made a feeble attempt at trying to snatch it back. She didn't mind really. These rituals were all part of the fun, and her friends knew that she didn't really want to keep it private – they always used to read each other's love letters. 'My darling Mary,' Audrey began. 'Ooo, I thought you didn't know this man. Well he thinks you're his darling!'

Mary blushed, but not because she'd been caught out. The truth was she didn't feel anything except pity for this man. She had met him on a train, they chatted and she had thought no more about it; after all, she would talk to anyone and everyone to pass the time on a long journey. She was being friendly; she certainly wasn't in love. In her mind you couldn't even call their exchange a flirtation. She knew what that felt like because she'd experienced it with Frank. He was but a fond memory now – a love affair squashed by the circumstances of war, she told herself.

Unfortunately, the sailor had other thoughts, as the passion expressed in his letter revealed.

'He says he loves you and he's coming to the camp,' Audrey squealed.

'Look – she's gone all red,' Marion teased. 'Gee, Mary, what happened?'

'Nothing, I tell you! It's all in his head!'

'Your trouble is you're too nice,' Beth remarked, offering a more removed perspective on the situation. 'You don't want to hurt his feelings just like you don't want to hurt anyone's feelings, but can't you see by doing that you're leading the poor boy on?'

'You weren't there, Beth. If she says she didn't lead him on then she didn't,' said Enid defensively.

Mary knew Beth was right in one sense – she hated being nasty to anyone – but she was wrong about leading him on. Still, it wasn't long before the focus was on someone else. Marion had a love letter of her own she wanted to share and, while Mary was thankful for the distraction, after a few minutes she never gave her letter or the sailor a second thought.

The next day it was back to work as normal, loading ten truckers up with food to deliver to the different Scottish regiments. Mary loved this part of the job because every day she would meet someone new, learn something or eat a food she'd never tried before.

'Today I had lunch with a bunch of Polish soldiers,' she enthused back at the billet. 'I couldn't understand a word they were saying but it was lovely.'

'Mary,' Beth interrupted.

'They had this funny beetroot like pickle, it was weird but it tasted ...'

'Mary, listen!' Beth insisted.

'What?'

'The military police are here to see you.'

'To see me? Why for goodness sake?'

Mary turned to see two stern officers walking towards her.

'What do you know about this man?' One of them asked, showing her a photograph.

'I don't know him.'

'Oh, I think you do. Take a closer look.'

Mary looked hard. 'He does seem a little familiar.'

'A little familiar?' The officer smirked, looking at his colleague. 'You were engaged to this man, weren't you?'

'What?' Suddenly it dawned on Mary from where she recognised his face – it was the sailor, the man who kept writing, declaring a love she couldn't fathom. 'I wasn't engaged to the man at all!'

'Really?' he said, accusingly. 'That's not what he told us. His mother told us the same story, so someone is lying. What do you have to say?'

'Look, I'm not calling anyone a liar, but I never agreed to marry him! I never even agreed to be engaged to him, and I certainly never met his mother!'

The sailor had gone AWOL and had been arrested at Edinburgh station on his way to find Mary. Mary explained that his mind must have been affected by the awful bombardment his ships had suffered and, as a result, his imagination was running riot. Eventually her truth was upheld and she was cleared of any involvement with his fleeing the navy, but it didn't stop his mother from visiting her in Perth, searching for answers.

For most people, the experience would have made them more cautious of talking to strangers in train carriages, but Mary never followed most people.

6

SOUL MATES

'What a day to start my holiday,' Mary thought, as she stood on the crowded platform. The Billiard Room Gang were there to wave her off for two weeks' leave back in Stockton; she was going to miss them. That was if she could find her way onto the train. Mary scanned the carriages. There were soldiers hanging out of every window and not a seat to be found.

The whistle blew. 'What are you waiting for, Mary? Get on!' Ella ordered, throwing Mary's suitcase onto a compartment as she spoke. Mary jumped on just as the train pulled away – trust Ella to be straight in there, she laughed.

The train was alive with stories and songs. There were soldiers everywhere, sitting on cases, standing in corridors – anywhere they could find space. What little air there was had been filled with cigarette smoke, so much as to become disorientating.

'I'm the only woman on this train,' Mary thought, suddenly feeling self-conscious. At least, she couldn't see any others. She now wished that Ella hadn't thrown her case so carelessly. How on earth was she going to find it?

'Would you like to sit here, sweetheart?' It was one of several offers Mary declined politely, as she squeezed through the carriages, scanning the floor and racks for her luggage. She spotted it eventually but, having found it, getting to it was another challenge. She made her way over, not lifting her eyes from it once in case it disappeared from sight again. Mary was so fixated on retrieving her case that she barely noticed the gentlemanly soldiers who moved to let her pass.

'Is this what you're looking for?' one asked her, lifting the case from the spot by his feet where it had landed.

'Yes, thank you,' Mary took it without looking up. She squeezed into a small space on the bench opposite, clutching the suitcase to her knees and began to relax.

The soldier who had passed her bag, didn't speak again for the rest of the journey. While the others, giddy with the excitement of going home, flirted and attempted to outdo each other with tales of bravery, he sat silent and still. Mary thought him a little aloof, yet, at the same time, was fascinated by his calm. He was beautiful, but she guessed he knew that. He didn't need to flirt with girls; she imagined that one flash of his white blonde hair from under his khaki beret was enough to grab their attention. It was enough to keep her interested anyway. That and his name, Butt. What kind of a name was that? Surely that wasn't it. It was painted on his bag, but she couldn't see round the twist to read the rest of it. He was a member of the Black Watch, she could tell that from the bright red feather in his hat. Judging by the colour of his skin he'd been serving overseas too. At least, she was certain you'd never get a tan like that living in Scotland.

It was an hour to Edinburgh, where Mary had to change trains. Once on the platform, she was back in her own world, focused only on finding her connection to Darlington and getting home for her fourteen days leave.

'Can I ask you something?' It was the soldier from the carriage. His voice startled Mary out of her daydream. Now he was standing, she noticed his height. He was taller than her, which she liked. Still, she reasoned, if he thought that she was going to simply melt at his beauty then he could think again. 'So, he decides to talk to me now,' she thought. At the same time, she was secretly pleased to have caught his attention; she just didn't want him to know that.

'Where you making for?' he asked.

Mary kept walking. 'You'll never have heard of it.'

'Well, I might. Where are you going?'

'You won't even know it, so what's the point in telling you?' she said, hurriedly.

Unruffled, he asked again. 'Go, on. You never know, I might know it.'

Mary looked at him, his blue eyes dancing, and she gave in. 'It's a little place called Stockton-on-Tees. Anyway, where do you come from?'

'Well you won't have heard of it either,' he teased.

'Why not?'

'Oh, because it's just a little place called Thornaby-on-Tees.'

'What? You are going to Thornaby?' Mary couldn't believe it, this exotic man going to Thornaby – surely not!

'Yes,' he said smiling.

'Well, good grief!'

'So, which stop do we get off?'

'You don't know, do you?' Mary asked, clocking the 'we' in his question.

'No. I haven't a clue.'

'Well, follow me, I know,' Mary announced, marching along the platform towards their train. The handsome Black Watch soldier followed her all the way. At least she was confident about the direction she was heading, even if her heart was moving into unknown territory.

On the subsequent journey, Mary learned that he was called John, and that the Butt she had found so peculiar earlier was only the first part of his surname, Butterwick. It was John's first time home in nine years. He had been serving in India as a boy soldier when war broke out, and that had put an end to what would have been normal annual leave from overseas.

It was almost four in the morning when the train reached Thornaby. The station was deserted, except for a lone milk float where Mary perched herself for the duration. When the next train would be coming for Stockton was anyone's guess.

'Thornaby's that way.' She pointed off behind her.

'Are you going to wait for a train?'

'I'll give it a bit.'

'You could be here hours.'

'Maybe,' she shrugged.

John stood there silently; Mary thought, what's he waiting for? I've told him where to go, but he didn't seem to be in a rush to get anywhere.

'Does your mother know you're coming home?' she asked.

'No, she hasn't a clue.'

'What?' Mary was stunned. 'You think you're going to go home at this time of a morning and get your mother out of bed when she's not expecting you – that's awful! You could give her a heart attack.'

'I hadn't thought about it that way,' he mused.

'Well, flipping heck, I'd be shocked! Wouldn't you?'

'We weren't allowed to tell anyone where we were.' He said it in such a matter-of-fact manner that Mary's heart went out to him.

'Tell you what – why don't you come home with me? My mother will cook you breakfast and then you can go home.'

'Won't your mother be shocked too?'

'No, she knows I'm coming home.'

'I mean, when she sees me?'

'Oh, goodness no, she's used to me bringing all manner of stray dogs home!'

John raised an eyebrow and smiled. 'So, I'm a stray dog now, am I?'

Mary stood up and shook her head. 'Come on.'

They walked under first light from Thornaby station to Mary's parents in Newtown. Talking to John, the distance seemed far less than she had remembered.

Just as she expected, Mary's parents asked few questions when they arrived home. Hilda's concern wasn't who this young man was but rather that her daughter was home safe and that she had a hearty start to the day. However, while waving John goodbye after breakfast, Mary knew inside that this stray dog wouldn't be gone for long; and nor would she want him to be.

Unfortunately for Mary, John's parents weren't quite so accommodating of their new courtship.

'Get out! I don't want anything to do with you!' his mother told her.

Mary went back several times to beg and plead with her future mother-in-law to come to the wedding, but she was resolute.

'Mary, it's not anything to do with you personally,' John reasoned. 'If we'd been the type of couple where I'd taken you home every Sunday afternoon for tea and scones, then she would be all right.'

'Yes, well we aren't, and as it is she's just hitting the roof,' Mary batted back, not knowing what to do to change it. Of course, she knew it must have been difficult for his mother – her son had walked back into her life after nine years, which must have been a shock in itself without him adding the news that he was to be married. It was difficult for her parents to comprehend the speed of their romance too, but, however uneasy they might have felt, at least they didn't block John out.

The two weeks' leave were soon up. Just days ago, Mary had thought that her separation from the Billiard Room Gang was hard. Little did she know that it was nothing compared to the longing she was to feel being separated from John. 'So this is what they call heartache,' she thought. She missed John like a part of her was gone, leaving a physical ache, a longing, in its place. Her heart felt like it was swelling with so much love that soon her chest would no longer be able to contain it. She couldn't wait to be Mrs Butterwick. They had a special licence to be married three months later, on 6 March at Stockton Parish Church. It seemed so rushed to everyone who knew them, but, for Mary, their wedding day couldn't come soon enough.

7

DODGING DEATH, EMBRACING LIFE

'You're a dark horse, Mary Wood,' Ella joked. 'Wait 'til Kingpin hears about this.'

Audrey, or Kingpin, as she was also affectionately called, was out doing what her nickname explained best. They found her in the yard, flat on her back, huge grease gun in hand, pumping away to keep the pins on her vehicle, and anyone else's which needed it, lubricated.

'Hey, Kingpin, look who I've found!'

Audrey rolled out from under the truck and grinned.

'So, you've found a man to steady those rubber legs?'

'News travels fast,' Mary laughed.

'Not as fast as you, lady,' Audrey bounced back, sitting up to face them. 'So, tell me – who is the lucky man?'

Mary didn't mind; indeed, she was bursting to tell anyone and everyone about John. This time, however, it was different. She didn't want to share his letters; those were his special words for her. At the same time, she didn't want to keep him a secret. John was a joy in her life and she wanted to share the happiness she felt at having found him.

Their courtship was fast, even for wartime, yet it never seemed rushed to them. During wartime death stalked every corner; the way Mary saw it, life could be short, so if you knew something was right in your heart, why wait?

John had been a Chindit, one of the allied Special Forces which operated deep behind enemy lines in North Burma. Time and again he had been dropped behind the Japanese lines, and for many months he lived and fought in the jungles of occupied Burma, completely reliant on airdrops for supplies.

He spoke little of what he'd seen, but he didn't need to. Mary knew it was a wonder he had made it home at all and, for that, she was all the more grateful. She was aware that John's war was a completely different war to the one she had experienced to date. Her role was transporting prisoners of war and taking care of British officers. The prisoners of war were hated like mosquitoes for what they represented, yet, isolated from their cause, they were men just the same and Mary tried to see the humanity in each one. The Italians, she believed, were big softies when you got to know them. They were creative too, she thought. Given a bit of tin or metal of any kind they would make a cigarette lighter or a cigarette case – anything to keep occupied.

On many nights, Mary would drive for hours along dark narrow roads to collect prisoners arriving at the station.

'Here, give these to John,' Kath said, throwing a couple of packets of cigarettes Mary's way. They were meant for the prisoners but keeping back the rationed tobacco was the only way the girls could show some disdain for the enemy.

Mary folded down the steel steps for the SS prisoners to climb into her ambulance.

'Heil Hitler!' one announced, snapping his boots together, his hand raised in a defiant salute.

'Get in!' Mary booted him through the open door. It wasn't like her to be violent but some things you just can't let go.

It was a bumpy ride. It was March and at that time of year in Scotland you could still find yourself thigh deep in snow. This night was cold but clear – one of those nights Kath, who was a native to these parts and accompanied her on the drive, would describe as too cold for snow, although Mary never understood what that meant.

The snow chains rattled on the ground as Mary drove, barely able to see the road ahead. Suddenly she lost control of the vehicle. The prisoners yelled as they fell against each other in the back. Then, almost as quickly as it had spun, the vehicle stopped with a jolt. Mary jumped out and took a few breaths, her heart pounding. A few feet further and the ambulance would have careered over the side of a bridge in the road, and goodness knows what was down below. It was all right for the driving instructor to say if you skid, pull this way or that, but, when it came to it, the ordeal was all over before she knew where she was.

Getting back in the driving seat, she looked at Kath, who was white with fear.

'It's okay, my good fairy is with us,' Mary smiled. How she stopped, she would never know, but hers was not to reason why.

'If we were cats that would've been one of our nine lives,' Kath said, still shaken. 'Someone's looking after you, Mary. Give me one of those cigarettes – I think I need it.'

Mary laughed, to disguise her stomach flipping. 'It's obviously not our time yet,' she quipped, revving the engine before driving slowly to the camp, knowing how easily it could have been.

★

'There's a letter for you, Mary!' Hilda shouted up the stairs. She felt happy to have her daughter home so soon after her last leave from the army, even if the circumstances weren't entirely to her pleasing.

Mary raced down the stairs. Maybe it was a note from John's mother? Perhaps she'd had second thoughts about the wedding?

Mary opened it and her heart sank. It was from Frank, her Grenadier Guard, writing from the battle of Monte Cassino in Italy.

'*My Darling Mary,*' it began.

That was enough. She was nobody's darling but John's. She was getting married tomorrow, and nothing or nobody was going to get in the way.

'Who is it from?' Hilda asked.

'Oh, no one important,' she replied hastily, pushing the letter into her pocket. It had been at least two years since she last heard from Frank and more than the same time again since she had last seen him. Why, of all days, did she have to get a letter from him now?

'What is it? Let's see!'

Mary opened the note and handed it to her mother.

'*My Darling Mary,*' she read.

'Okay, Mother – I know what it says, I don't need to hear it out loud!' She didn't need to, the words were already etched onto her brain – words she wished she'd never read and, indeed, had never been written.

My Darling Mary,

I cannot tell you of some of the horrors I have seen here on this mountain. All that keeps me going is the thought of you.

There is not a day – no, less, an hour – goes by when I do not think of you.

The way I think of it is: who would I like to be the mother of my children? It is you, Mary and as soon as I come home I've decided I want you to be my wife.

Write when you can.

Yours always,

Frank.

'Well, blow me!' Hilda sighed sympathetically.

'What am I supposed to do, Mother? I'm getting married tomorrow.'

'Does this make any difference? Do you still want to marry John?'

'Of course I still want to marry John! How can you say that?'

'It's all right, stay calm!'

'I am calm,' she huffed, clearly not.

'Well, I suggest you write by return of post to this man and let him know, in no uncertain terms, that you are to be married.'

'How can I? It will hurt him so much; you've read what he said.'

'I know, dear, which is all the more reason why you need to tell him now. You don't want the poor man waiting for months, only to come home and find the woman he's been dreaming of has married someone else.'

'Why, what could I have done to make him think such a thing?'

'You don't need to have done anything, but you do need to respond and put an end to this right now.'

The Second World War touched everyone, but, within that shared experience, there were so many others, often too difficult to comprehend. Mary couldn't imagine what life must have been like for Frank, writing from the battlefield; Monte Cassino was a mountain which was fought over several times during the war – it must have seemed such a waste of life. She could not tell how long ago he had written the letter. She tried to imagine how far his proposal had travelled to reach her and the long journey her refusal still had to make. Would he even be alive to read her reply?

Aside from the initial shock on opening the letter, Mary was flattered by its sentiment – that such a handsome, brave and gallant man would want her to be his wife. Lifting her pen, she knew what she had to say would be hurtful and difficult. It was for her too; Frank was her first love and in that sense would always be special.

She smiled, remembering how this tall Grenadier Guard would turn heads as they walked hand in hand down Stockton High Street. She had felt so lucky to have his attention. Yet that love seemed a world away from what she felt in her heart now. Here she was, on the eve of her wedding, with a choice between two handsome soldiers, but, for Mary, it was not an option. Yes, she had used that same four letter word to describe her emotions for both men, but, inside, although she struggled to describe it, she knew her feelings were not the same. It wasn't just that her feelings for Frank had changed. This time it was different, she just knew. Her future life with John seemed so set, so right; no matter what offers were to come her way, there was no alternative, and she wouldn't want there to be.

8

MR AND MRS

Mary was 20 when she said 'I do', to become Mrs Butterwick. Her vows were taken in army uniform, opposite her brave Black Watch soldier and her love. The ceremony was simple – there was no money for extravagance, no presents, no dress and no party, yet for Mary the day was perfect.

It had begun with a disappointment; a telegram arrived to say that the best man, John's brother, Fred, was unable to make it. He wasn't to arrive home from service for another couple of days, but the reasons why were confidential. They later learned that he was being dropped into the battle and all leave for his regiment had been cancelled.

Mary's brother, Jack, stepped into the role and, although John's brother was unable sadly to make it, there was much joy when his mother did. Mary was also delighted that her friends Kath, Enid and Ella were all able to secure leave to join her as bridesmaids, all dressed, like the bride, in army uniform – it was all the clothes they had. The reception party enjoyed a cup of tea and sponge cake at Mary's parents' home, before the newlyweds headed off on honeymoon: a couple of days visiting John's grandmother in Crook, in County Durham, and another few days in Manchester with Mary's aunt, Edith.

Everything, and yet nothing, had changed. A week later, John was back with his regiment in Glasgow and Mary returned to the Billiard Room.

Life in Scotland was as fun-filled as ever with the girls, but Mary no longer found the attention from soldiers as innocent and amusing as she once had. She particularly wasn't keen on driving officers in the 'bug car', which was so small that she couldn't fit in without her knees riding up against the steering wheel. Nevertheless, if a job came in you had to get on and do it.

'I can't do it this time,' Mary thought to herself on one occasion. 'That guy thinks he's the bee's knees. He's always feeling women's legs in the car, and I'm sick of it!'

Despite her gut instinct, she did take him. Sure enough, it wasn't long before his hand slipped onto her knee.

'I should remind you I'm a married woman, Officer,' she warned.

He continued defiantly until Mary stopped the car with a jolt, announcing: 'We're here now.'

It was part of the protocol that the driver jumped out of the car, walked around the front of the vehicle and saluted the officer as he got out.

Wedged in behind the steering wheel, Mary could barely move as it was, so she didn't. The officer stared at her.

'I can hardly move here, so it'll be quicker if you open the door yourself,' she offered.

'I think you should remember your station and open the door.'

'I think you should've remembered your status before you started feeling my leg,' she bounced back.

The officer got out of the car and slammed the door behind him.

The following day, Mary was put on 'jankers' – official army punishment – for failing to salute an officer correctly. It required her to be confined to barracks, where she was given a long list of tedious tasks to keep her busy and ensure she wasn't tempted to commit the same offence again. When John heard about it he offered to take leave and jump on the first train to Perth. 'They'll have to let you off if I come,' he wrote to her. Mary thought his reaction sweet, but not realistic. In her view, she had disobeyed an officer so she'd have to pay for it.

'This is ridiculous, Corporal, it's pouring with rain!' Mary reasoned, when asked to wash windows during a downpour as part of her punishment while on jankers.

'I don't care,' came the response. 'Out you go!'

It would have been simpler to have just opened the door and saluted that brute of an officer, but things were always easier with hindsight, and, given her time again, she probably still would have snubbed him.

The water was running into the house from loose tiles on the porch roof, and forming more puddles as quickly as Mary could dry them. It was a thankless task. She could be on her hands and knees mopping all day and it wouldn't make any difference.

'You've done a grand job there, girl!'

It couldn't be, surely not. She looked up: it was John! Her heart leapt – he had come to save her.

Just as he said he would, John did get Mary off jankers that night, and became a life long friend of the Billiard Room Gang as a result.

The girls were also very grateful for the extra money coming in from Mary's marriage allowance, which, as with everything else, was shared. It wasn't a fortune; it simply paid for a night out and a packet of cigarettes, but anything to make the days pass more enjoyably was a welcome treat.

However, although on the surface they seemed happy to accept her new married status, over the past few weeks Mary had begun to notice something a little odd about the way her room mates were treating her. It was as if they wanted her wrapped in cotton wool. At first, Audrey wouldn't hear of Mary getting under the vehicle to grease the springs. Still, she didn't think too much about it because Audrey was Kingpin after all. But when Kath also started – 'Don't be lifting that, Mary, I'll do it!' – she wondered what was up. Surely it couldn't be that they were now all worried in case something happened to her and they lost her marriage allowance?

'One's enough for you tonight, rubber legs!' Ella joked as Mary gave in her order for a port and lemon.

'What? Have we spent up already?'

'No, but …' Ella stumbled.

'So, it's just me who can't have one? Well, thanks very much girls! I'm still standing aren't I?'

'I think we could all be doing with getting back a little earlier tonight,' Kath suggested. 'We need to get to that coal stack while there is still some there. It looked a bit depleted yesterday.'

Mary pulled her face and, reluctantly, they all headed back to the house.

'All right, where's the bucket?' Mary asked.

'You can't get the coal,' Ella said quickly.

'Why on earth not? What's all this pussy-footing around me? I'm fed up of it!'

'We're only thinking of you, Mary,' Ella said, looking hurt.

'What are you talking about?'

'Well, when are you going to report for your towels?' Ella piped up. Sanitary towels were kept in a box under the bed. Everyone knew when the others needed them because you had to go and ask for them, something Mary hadn't done for three months.

'So?'

'So – you could be pregnant,' Kath said, matter-of-fact.

'What?'

'Having a baby, you daft lump!' Audrey added.

'How does that happen then?' Mary asked innocently.

Kath and Enid started shouting instructions at her across the room while the others fell about laughing, but Mary didn't see what was so funny. How was she to know where babies came from? Kath and Enid only knew that because they'd been nurses, she thought.

When Mary did have to ask for her towels a couple of weeks later, there was commotion again. Mary was later to learn that she'd had an early miscarriage, but at the time she couldn't understand what all the fuss was about.

9

CIVVY STREET

The end of World War II was a time of great jubilation across the country. Yet, while Mary joined in the euphoria of victory, her change in circumstances aroused unexpected sadness.

'What are you crying for, you big daft lump? You're going home,' Kath reasoned.

'I know,' Mary sniffed.

'I don't know! The world is at peace, you've got a lovely husband to go home to and you've just been moved from a Wood to a Butterwick so you get to go home first! I think you should be laughing, not crying, dear girl,' Audrey added.

'I know,' Mary sniffed again, barely able to get her words out. The others were making light of it, but they understood too what was causing Mary's tears. It was a mixed emotion which they all felt. Being demobbed was not just the end of the war, but the end of their lives together. Hopefully it wouldn't be the end of their friendship, but who knew where life would take them now?

Mary's parents made up a room in their house as a home for her and John to live in. However, with John still in the army, trying to create their home separate from her parents' life didn't feel real. To Mary, used to living surrounded by friends, it felt as if she was living in a bed-sit, and only exacerbated the loneliness she felt on leaving the gang behind. She found herself living for the days when John would come home on leave, and pining while he was away. Before now, Mary had been married but knew little of married life. Yes, she'd worked out where babies came from, but there was much still to learn.

'Always put your bill money to one side every week,' her mother taught her, 'because if you can't put it away for one week, you're never going to be able to find enough money for two weeks.'

Mary followed that rule with diligence and it was just as well, because if it wasn't for the money John gave to Mary, he never would have had any.

'Have you got any money left, by chance?' John asked, every time he came home.

'Where's *your* money?' Mary asked in return, knowing full well what the answer would be. Well, there might be some variation in the tale of who he'd given it to, but it would always be a similar sob story he'd been drawn into. A soldier would spin him a yarn about not seeing his wife and family for however long, and John would end up paying the man's train fare and then hitchhiking all the way from Southampton to Teesside himself. Worse than the money, in Mary's eyes, was the fact that John, who was in charge of the guard house, would regularly let soldiers out without leave to see their wives.

'But Mary, what would the poor guy have been doing in that camp?' he'd reason.

'For goodness sake, John, when are you going to grow up and realise? You've come away, so you expect that they should just be able to waltz off too. One of these days one of them won't come back!'

Of course, that did happen occasionally and John had to admit that his men were AWOL. He'd win stripes and then lose them overnight, but it never stopped his heart strings from being pulled. No rules could dissuade him from doing what he believed was a good turn.

Mary soon grew tired of being apart and, taking the matter into her own hands, jumped on a train to Southampton, where she found herself a live-in job, cleaning at a sea-front boarding house.

The house was run by a fearsome Austrian woman, Mrs Gold-berger, who ruled with a hysterical edge and spent what seemed like every penny she had doting on her nine-year-old daughter, Astrid. Whatever Astrid wanted, she got. She was the queen of the boarding house, and she knew it. Mary felt sorry for the child; being so spoiled, how else was she to turn out if not a brat? On the other hand, Mary often found the girl so irritating that she would rush to her room to calm down save she gave the youngster a piece of her mind.

It wasn't so much the child's bad manners that annoyed Mary, although she couldn't ever imagine having spoken to an adult while growing up the way Astrid would speak to her. It was more frustration at seeing all the money coming in seemingly being spent on treats, such as taking Astrid skating, while the house, in dire need of repair, fell apart around them.

Mary lived in a tiny attic room at the front of the house, in which no amount of cleaning could disguise the crumbling walls and broken floorboards. Every morning, she'd lie and watch the daylight dance across the room in all directions as it seeped through innumerable cracks in the tiles. It wasn't ideal, but for Mary it was better than being stuck at home while John was hundreds of miles away. At least this way she could see him every weekend.

Mary hadn't expected the staff living quarters to be anything special. She had, however, expected the guest accommodation to be a little more presentable, especially as it was being used to house naval officers. Yes, times were hard, but Mary found the lack of care unforgivable. In her mind, there was no excuse for the dust, which had been allowed to gather for what seemed like years. It was clear that no attention was being paid to the upkeep of the house. There was no carpet, only under-felt covering the floors throughout, even in the sitting room. This was the complete opposite of what Mary had been used to for the past six-and-a-half-years. In the army, she knew exactly what was expected of her and exactly what she needed to do. Now she spent most of her time feeling horrified at how low standards had sunk.

'Aarrghhhh!' Mary shrieked on more than one occasion, jumping back as she pulled off a bed sheet to find a mattress riddled with cockroaches. It felt wrong that the authorities paid good money for servicemen to live in such squalor. Not only that but Mrs Goldberger would make twice as much by renting a room to one naval officer at night and the same room to another man in the day.

'This isn't right!' Mary challenged her.

'What are you talking about now?' Mrs Goldberger asked, dismissively.

'There are personal belongings in these drawers and you are letting other people use the rooms.'

'If they want to leave items in the drawer, that's up to them. It's nothing to do with me.'

'But these are gold braids we're talking about – naval captains. I think they deserve more respect than to have their beds slept in by strangers while they are out working.'

'What about *my* respect, from *you*?'

'I'm only saying …'

'Well, don't!' Mrs Goldberger interrupted, throwing her hands in the air dramatically, as she was want to do when anything did not go her way. 'You're not paid to speak, you're paid to clean,' she added sharply, making clear to Mary that that was to be the end of the conversation.

To Mary, the mean spiritedness of Mrs Goldberger was magnified further by John's generosity. While Mrs Goldberger cut every corner she could to make an extra shilling, John would be handing out his last penny to any stranger in need. For Mrs Goldberger, everything was business; there was no such thing as good will. If John wanted to stay over at the weekend, she would charge for bed and breakfast. Any meals on top of that had to be paid for too, leaving Mary with very little wages after these deductions had been made.

'Where is the rest of my money, Mrs Goldberger?' Mary asked innocently, on opening her first wage packet to find only two shillings.

'Count it up and I'm sure you'll find it's right,' she said abruptly.

'But you said I'd get …'

'Yes, but your man stayed one night, and then there was his breakfast and tea to pay for,' she jumped in.

'His tea? Two sardines on toast and a couple of spoonfuls of baked beans! How much can that cost? Besides which, it's hardly tea enough for a man!'

'It's what everyone gets round here. If you don't like it you know what you can do,' Mrs Goldberger said, arms in the air again, preparing for a dramatic exit. As she walked away, she hollered without turning: 'Oh, and by the way, you owe me for a bar of soap – I'll take that from next week's wages unless you want to pay before.'

It was several months before John was finally demobbed, leaving the army with £12 in his pocket and a demob suit.

The couple returned home to Teesside, moving back into the room at Mary's parents' home. It wasn't easy to find a job when all you'd known was being a soldier at war, but John had an added reason to find work now – it looked like the couple were soon to have a family of their own. Both excited and nervous, they decided to go to the doctors together to find out.

'Congratulations, Mrs Butterwick, you're expecting a baby,' the doctor told her. Mary was beaming – this was wonderful news.

Walking home down Stockton High Street, she heard a man shout 'John!' and, the next thing she knew, he was running towards them and embracing her husband in a huge bear hug. Surely he couldn't know their good news already, she thought, bewildered.

'You don't know what this fella of yours did for me!' he said, excitedly.

Mary looked on, speechless – 'This man is a nutcase,' she thought.

'It's okay, mate,' John said calmly. 'Good to see you, Jock.'

'No, let me tell her,' he enthused. 'I owe my life to this man.'

Jock told the story of how the two of them had been behind Japanese lines. If any soldiers went down with an illness, and so many did, they were propped up beside a tree and given a revolver. There were three options – wait until you starved to death, risk being captured or shoot yourself. Rather than hand his friend a revolver, John risked his own safety by putting him on his back and carrying him for miles until they reached base.

'You name it, I had it – typhoid, malaria, dysentery ...' Jock continued. 'If John hadn't have done what he did, I would be a dead man for sure.'

Mary was overwhelmed both by this man's emotion and her own. He spoke of a man she did not know, of horrors she'd never understand and would probably never wish to. Yes, John was her hero – he was her love, her husband, and would soon be the father of her child. Yet this man spoke of a different heroism. This was the kind of heroism she could only imagine, the type they make films about.

As they walked away, she asked: 'Is that true, John? Is what that man said really true?'

'Yes, Mary, it is,' he answered quietly.

'You really did that!' Mary said, excitedly, but her giddiness found no companion.

John brushed it off modestly. 'That's just what we did, Mary.'

As Mary was to learn over the years, that was John: laid back and reserved. Whatever his fears were, he kept them well hidden.

10

MONKEY BUSINESS

Once John found work, as a guard on the railway, the couple set about trying to find a home of their own. However, with houses being filled quicker than they could be built, it appeared that they could be in for a long wait. Houses were provided on a points system. The more years you had served in the army and the more children you had, the more points you got. Even though Mary and John had both served in the army, it still took two years before they were offered a home, by which time their first child, Keith, was born, and their second was on its way.

'We've been offered a house, John!' Mary beamed, holding up the letter from the council as if to prove that it was real, that it was happening at last.

'Let me look?' he asked, smiling.

'It's in Ragworth – one of the new houses,' Mary added excitedly, as John read the letter. 'It's our home, John, our first proper home.' John lifted her up and swung her round – this news caused for a celebration.

The house was indeed new, so new that next door was still being built when they moved in. It didn't take long for the neighbours to arrive – as soon as the bath was in, the house was rented to another young couple also expecting a child.

Wartime rationing of goods, which also worked on a points system, was still in place, meaning that buying anything wasn't simply about having enough money to purchase it. Everyone had so many points to spend in the form of coupons, which had to be handed over to the shopkeeper as well as the money.

Household textiles came under the points for clothing allowance, and Mary didn't have enough spare to buy curtains. Learning to make do with what they had, she dyed a pair of sheets, given as a belated wedding present, and pinned them up at the sitting room window.

'What do you think?' Mary asked John, stepping back from her handiwork.

'It looks just grand, Mary – you make everything beautiful.'

Mary felt a smile grow from her very core and fill her whole body with joy. The baby moved inside her, as if leaping with excitement too; this was going to be a good year.

It wasn't long before John and Mary made friends with their neighbours, Charlie and Alice. Soon after that, John being John, he was talked easily into helping out on Charlie's latest business scheme, selling tropical fish and exotic animals.

Before long, their sitting room became like a stock room, always full of fish tanks to be glazed and sealed. Mary would help by typing out all the business letters and envelopes, as well as putting together little packets of fish food. After a day's work on the railway, John would come home, grab a quick meal and then be out with Charlie, often driving through the night to London and back, collecting stock for the shops.

One day, John came home carrying the biggest snake Mary had ever seen.

'Right, this will have to go in the bath until I can take it away,' he said, matter-of-factly, leaving Mary standing, open-mouthed, at the door. Then, just when she thought it couldn't get worse, Mary arrived home to find three monkeys swinging on the lights in the sitting room.

'John!' she shouted, slamming the door shut on their unusual visitors.

'It's just until tomorrow when Charlie can drop them off to their new owners. Don't be worrying about them – they're meant to be pets, they won't do you any harm,' he explained.

'Pets! A dog, a cat – that's what I call a pet! Monkeys! Whoever heard of a pet monkey?'

'You'll be surprised what people keep as pets these days, Mary.'

'Surprised? Too right I'm surprised – it's not every day you come home to find three monkeys taking over the house.'

'Oh, come on now, Mary. You know, we've got another baby coming, we've got to make money the best way we can.'

Mary sighed with frustration. 'Well, I don't see much money coming our way from this.'

'Well, these things take time, Mary. When things get really good, I'll become a director and we'll get it then.'

Mary shook her head and was about to disagree when there was a knock on the wall.

'Oh, what now?' she said wearily.

'It's next door; they're probably wanting us to keep it down,' John suggested.

There was another bang – this time louder, followed by what sounded like a muffled cry for help. Mary looked out of the window. 'Where's Charlie's car?'

'I don't know. He must be out.'

'Oh, goodness – Alice!' Alice was prone to asthma attacks, sometimes so bad that she didn't have the strength to go upstairs to get her inhaler. Many times when the men were at work, Alice would bang on the wall of whichever room she was in. On hearing this, Mary would take Keith in her arms and race next door. The inhaler was, thankfully, always in the same spot, in the top drawer of the dressing table. Mary would run upstairs get the inhaler and wait with Alice until her wheezing settled or, if she didn't seem to be getting better within a few minutes, Mary would call the doctor and try to hide her anxiety while waiting for him to arrive.

Mary opened the door to hear a cry so primal it shocked her.

'Alice!'

'Mary, thank goodness you're here!'

Mary went to run upstairs to get the inhaler. 'Mary, it's the baby – the baby's coming.'

'Okay – stay calm! I'm going to go and get the midwife.'

'No, don't leave me, Mary, please,' Alice pleaded. Mary looked at her, she couldn't leave her, but how could she deliver a baby? She wouldn't know the first thing to do.

'Then let me get John and he can get the midwife,' Mary suggested, trying to stay calm while Alice gave out another earthy cry.

'Don't leave me, Mary! My waters have broken; I can feel the baby coming.'

Mary banged on the wall for John and tried to get Alice upstairs to the bed.

'What's going on, Mary, are you okay?' John shouted through the front door, unable to see the pair struggling up the stairs.

'It's the baby, John! It's on its way! Can you fetch the midwife and try to find Charlie?'

'You've had a baby, Mary – tell me what I should do?' Alice asked, looking for reassurance that the pain would ease.

Having a baby and delivering a baby are two completely different things, thought Mary. She could remember very little about her own experience. She must have been in a lot of pain, but when the midwife handed her Keith and she saw his little face smiling up at her, it was as if nothing else mattered. She helped Alice onto the bed and rubbed her head gently. 'Remember to breathe, make sure you push with the contractions, and we'll be saying 'Hello' to your new baby before we know it.'

By the time the midwife arrived the baby's head was already showing, and Mary stayed to help with the delivery.

'It's a girl!' she announced excitedly, handing the newborn to its mother with tears in her eyes.

'It'll be your turn soon,' the midwife smiled, looking at Mary's seven-month bump.

'Two months to go,' said Mary.

'You did well today. Have you delivered a baby before?'

'Never, it was quite the experience,' she laughed.

'Yes – I've gotten used to it now, but watching you made me think back to my first time.'

'It's a marvel to behold,' Mary beamed.

'New life always is. I'm more used to the mechanics of it now, but a baby's first cry – it gets me every time.'

Two months later, Mary too had a baby girl, Carol. It was good to have a friend close by who was experiencing the same joys. The two families grew together and, before long, both women were mothers of four. However, in terms of wealth, the families were growing further apart by the day.

'What do you think?' Alice asked, holding her wrist up to show off a new watch.

'Is that real gold?' Mary asked.

'Yes – of course, it's real gold! 24 carat! I've got a certificate to prove it,' she laughed.

'My goodness, you'd better not lose that.'

'Do you like it?'

'Alice, it's beautiful,' Mary replied, genuinely. 'I wish you health to wear.'

Alice beamed. She had so many gifts from Charlie these days. If it wasn't a watch, it was a new diamond ring or a cashmere coat. Mary knew it was only natural that Charlie would want to treat his wife with such luxuries and she didn't begrudge that, but it did stick in the throat a little when John was working all hours to help the business grow and they were still struggling to get by on £7 a week. It wasn't so much that she couldn't afford the same luxuries as Alice – she didn't want the money for herself. It was when it came to the children that the differences hurt the most.

At Christmas, Alice and Charlie bought four new bikes, one for each of their children. The Butterwick bunch would have been delighted with new bikes as well, except there was no way the budget, even with cutbacks in other areas, would stretch that far. If Mary had £1 left over at the end of the week, after putting money aside for rent, insurances and food, then she considered herself very wealthy.

There was always hire purchase, but that went against everything Mary believed in. In her view, if you didn't have the money to pay for something outright then you just had to do without. As a family they rarely had the money for treats, and, with John working so much, he didn't have the time to lavish on them either. Sometimes a week would go by without John seeing the children – they would be in bed before he came home, and he'd be out in the morning before they woke.

Eventually, John gave up his job on the railway to work as a salesman for Charlie full time. Unfortunately this didn't see John working any fewer hours than before because, by this time, Charlie had accumulated a chain of shops, from Stockton stretching north to Consett in County Durham, and John worked between all of them.

In an attempt to keep some semblance of family life, Mary insisted on eating Sunday dinner as a family. Even that had to work around the Quayside market at Newcastle, but Mary found a compromise and would cook the meal at teatime to make sure they could all sit down and eat together.

'What are we doing all this for, John?' Mary asked wearily. 'Tell me exactly, because I need to know.'

'Don't worry. I'll be a director soon and we'll see the fruits of it then.'

'I don't know. I question that, John, I really do.'

'The business is growing, Mary. Charlie is starting a car hire firm soon – once that's set up then we'll start to see the benefits too.'

'Oh, whatever next, John? Where and how far is he going to go, because there are only so many hours in the day?'

'He's given me his word, Mary,' John said, as if signalling an end to the conversation, and Mary knew there was no point in pushing it any further. She only went along with it because, in her mind, that is what you did in a marriage, but it was getting to the point where she could stand it no longer. As far as she could see, John was not and had never been in Charlie's plan.

Charlie and Alice now lived in a huge farm house, so they were no longer neighbours and barely even friends.

'I want to go on holiday, John,' she said, changing the subject.

'Okay,' he agreed.

'I mean all of us together, as a family.'

'I'll have to see what's on at work, but if you want to take the kids …'

'We're all going,' Mary interrupted. 'These children don't know you. They are not getting to know their father, and you're not getting to know them. It's not on.'

'Okay, okay. We'll go away – you find something and I'll sort it with work.'

There was no more discussion to be had, but Mary was satisfied. No doubt she would have to organise the holiday herself, but at least if John hadn't noticed the distance his work had put between them all, he knew it now. More than that, he knew that Mary wasn't going to let the family drift apart. If it did, there'd be trouble.

11

OLD FRIENDS

Scotland always held a special place in Mary's heart. She loved the openness, the fresh air, the stillness, the rugged coast and the memories of her army days with the Billiard Room Gang. Spending time there was bound to bring the family closer together, she thought. Mary bought a second-hand tent, to try out the family's taste for camping. She loved the idea of being free, setting up home wherever the fancy took.

'That looks fantastic, Mary,' John enthused, when she showed him. 'Charlie says we can have a car to get us there.'

'He'll want paying for that, but that's up to you.'

'Mary, he said we could have it,' he said, irritated at her cynicism. 'Besides, I'm managing all these vehicles, why shouldn't I have one for a couple of weeks?'

Everything was set for the family to go, then, two days before the holiday, John came home crestfallen.

'If we're going to Scotland, we'll have to find another way of getting there, Mary,' he said quietly.

'What?'

'Charlie says that he's booked out the car he promised us to someone else, so we can't have it. I'm sorry.'

'"Sorry?" We've got four kids here all excited about going on holiday; does he think we can just tell them "Sorry"?'

'He's let us down, Mary, I know that,' he said wearily. 'But don't worry, we'll get there somehow.'

Mary was livid, but she could see from John's face how hurt he was and she didn't want to add to that. John's friendship with Charlie, his dream of being a company director and his job all ended that day.

Perhaps it was the disappointment of being let down, or perhaps it was simply that time had passed quicker than she'd ever imagined it could, but Mary longed to see her old Billiard Room Gang again. John sensed this and surprised her by borrowing a car from a friend. She never asked who it was or what he needed to do to repay the favour. Now wasn't a time for questions. John had lots of friends and was always generous; if someone wanted to treat him for once, she wasn't going to argue.

'Why don't we try to find Kath while we're in Scotland?' John suggested.

'Really?' Mary asked, the joy in her heart lighting her face at the thought of it.

John smiled, 'Yes, why not?'

'Well, I don't have her address,' she hesitated, not wanting to put any obstacles between John's hope and a reunion with her friend. 'But I guess there's no harm in trying.'

Scotland was everything that Mary had remembered, and the children took to camping like it was an adventure. After such a struggle to keep everything together, it felt like they were a real family again. Everyone had a job to do to, be it fetching water or clearing the dishes, and they all pulled together. In the evening, Mary cooked a warming supper of corned beef hash and, while they ate, John told fantastic made-up stories of struggle and heroics, friendship and honour, which had the children hanging on his every word. Mary enjoyed them too, although she often thought that there was much true experience behind the tales, as if it was John's way of exorcising ghosts of his time as a Chindit in the war. Of course, he never relayed the horrors of this time to their children, or to anyone else as far as she was aware, but the places he described and the action heroes he created were surely borne of his army days.

They pitched up at a campsite in Kath's home town of Wick, which was the last main town before John O'Groats. It was a part of Scotland Mary was unfamiliar with. With the exception of her wedding, the girls were never given leave at the same time, so, while she knew the towns where each of her friends lived by name, Mary had never visited them.

Wick was a beautiful fishing town, with a lively harbour and a river running right through its centre. When they arrived, the place was dancing to the sound of brass bands marching down the streets. It felt like a celebratory fanfare and, in her mind's eye, Mary half expected Kath to be standing in the middle of the High Street waiting to greet her. She stopped everyone she could to ask: 'Do you know where Kath Sutherland lives?'

After three days of searching, Mary walked into the police station and enquired if anyone had any information on her friend. The officer gave her a look that said he thought she was crazy and sent her on her way no wiser as to Kath's whereabouts.

'We're going to have to go back home, John, because we've tried everything we can. There isn't really anywhere else to go,' Mary said, despondently.

She tried to keep upbeat for the children – it was their holiday too, after all. However, she couldn't hide her deep disappointment from John. After the ritual bedtime story, Mary got the children settled into bed and relaxed with her knitting while John strolled down to the local pub for a swift pint.

The comedown from not seeing Kath had left Mary weary, and she was asleep by the time John returned. The next morning she woke to the sound of him whistling and the smell of fried sausages drifting into the tent.

'I'm thinking, how about we stay here for another night?' he smiled.

'Yay!' the children all cheered in unison, while Mary looked at him incredulously.

Passing her breakfast, he whispered: 'I think I know where to find Kath.'

'What?' Mary could hardly contain her excitement. 'How come? What's happened?'

'Well,' he sat back, as if about to begin one of his stories. 'When I was in the pub last night I got talking to this fella …'

'Come on – have you seen her?' Mary couldn't wait for a tale to be told, she just wanted to know: had he seen Kath or not?

'No, let me finish,' he smiled. 'I got talking to this fella, and telling him what we were doing here, that we were looking for your friend, Kath, and how it looked like it might be a wasted trip, when he said: "That'll not be Kathy of the school bus, by any chance?"

'Now, I said that we didn't know anything about a school bus, and this girl isn't called Sutherland, but she is married, so that would account for that, and she is about the right age and fits the description.'

'So what do we do now?'

'Well, it might not be her, but I've got directions from this man for a village called Keiss, about twelve miles north of here. He says that's where we'll find Kathy of the school bus and hopefully she'll be the Kath we're looking for.'

She *was* the Kath they were looking for, now married, also with four children. So much had happened since the war years, but the feelings hadn't changed. As soon as Kath opened the door, Mary's arms flung open and the pair embraced. Being so young, Mary supposed they'd all taken their friendship for granted. Yet, back on civvy street she realised that such bonds were hard to find and harder to maintain. John and the children were her world now, but her friendship with the Billiard Room Gang was an important part of her too; seeing Kath again made her realise just how much.

'Promise me you'll never lose touch again,' Mary said, blinking back tears.

'You soft lump,' Kath laughed. 'I never went anywhere! I always knew your rubber legs would come bouncing back this way one of these days.'

Part 2

COPING WITH
THE UNIMAGINABLE

12

THE UNIMAGINABLE HAPPENS

February 1979 – the tabloids called it the winter of discontent, as severe weather froze the land while public sector strikes paralysed services. It turned many hearts to ice, but many more were broken. Mary's was one of them.

Looking up at the night sky, she prayed: 'Dear God, what is happening to the world? I've been told there are no ambulances to take John to hospital. He's sick, God, and I don't know how to help. The doctor won't come out either. Where is the care? Please help me! I'd take him to hospital myself, but I'm not strong enough to carry him to the car and he's in no state to get in on his own.'

'Thank goodness for her family,' she thought. Earlier that evening, in desperation, she had called her daughter, Carol, to ask if her son-in-law, Tony, would come and help dress John and lift him into the car. It was quite a shock for both of them to realise just how serious his illness had become. For Carol, it was the first she knew that her father was sick, and, for Mary, she had to admit that whatever it was that was wrong with him, John needed help that she couldn't give. Outside, snow had covered everything white as far as she could see. The street looked so calm, but Mary couldn't see any beauty, only a ghostly desolation. She thought that the streets must be empty because anyone with any sense was staying indoors. The roads and the pavements were treacherous. It was as if the change in weather was freezing everything, even life itself. Mary looked at the clock – had it really only been ten minutes since she called Carol? It seemed like forever, but she could only wait and hope and pray that Tony would be able to make it through the snow.

'Please, God, bring Tony here safely so that he can help me,' she pleaded. 'If you let this happen, if Tony comes, I promise I will do anything.'

John's illness had come on suddenly. Mary couldn't comprehend that in the morning everything had been fine, as it always had been, yet by the afternoon her world had changed and, no matter what she did, she couldn't get it back to how it was. Yes, the rubbish was piling up outside and money didn't seem to be going as far as it used to, but this current state of affairs was more of a nuisance to Mary than anything else; politics had never really interested her. Now she couldn't escape it. But, for Mary, this wasn't about politics – it was about the very fabric of her life.

When John came home from work that day, something had happened that had changed her husband beyond recognition. It wasn't right that he should be ill. He was never ill. She was the one who he was always worrying about, not the other way around. What was worse was the lack of help and care. This wasn't wartime anymore. The country now had a national health service, but without simple care and humanity, what did that mean?

She closed her eyes, wanting to visualise John well, but all she could see was his strained expression, all colour drained from his face as he told her he'd done a terrible thing.

'What do you mean you've done a terrible thing?' Mary asked, almost shouting. She couldn't believe he'd done anything bad, but she'd never seen him like this before. His army years in India had left him with a rugged, suntanned look, even in winter, but now, standing in the living room, visibly shaken, he was grey like she'd never seen him before.

'I've broken the wing mirror, driving the car into the garage.'

'Oh,' Mary sighed, exasperated. 'Is that it?'

He repeated it again: 'Putting the car into the garage – I've knocked the wing mirror off.'

'For goodness sake, what're the odds? It's a flaming wing mirror.'

'But that's not the point.'

'Well, what is the point? Sit down and tell me what the point is?'

John didn't respond to Mary's heightened emotion. Although obviously distressed, he just sat down slowly, which only worried her more.

'I can see everything about six times,' he said wearily. 'I didn't know which one was the right one and after I drove the car in, I realised I had knocked the wing mirror off.'

'You can see six? Six of what?'

'Six of everything!'

'So you're telling me that sitting there now, you can see six of me?'

'Yes – you've got one outline after another.'

'Well there's something wrong with your eyes then. Get on the phone to the optician!'

'Mary – not now. He'll be closed.'

'Well how are you going to drive to work like that? You can't, it's dangerous.'

'I understand that but I can't cope with this now. I'll ring him in the morning.'

Morning came, and John's eyesight hadn't improved. He put the phone down. 'He said it'll be six weeks.'

'Six weeks! You can't cope with that for six weeks! I'll phone my optician and ask if he can see you.'

Mary managed to get John an appointment that afternoon. He came out holding an envelope to take to the doctor, so Mary drove him straight there and they sat in the waiting room until he could be seen.

Noticing that John was carrying something as he left the surgery, Mary asked: 'What's that? Not the same envelope, I hope?'

'No,' John clearly didn't have the energy for all these questions but it only fired Mary up even more to get something done. 'The doctor has written this letter out. He wants me to put a stamp on it and put it in the pillar box so that it gets off today.'

'In other words he's saying that it's got to go immediately.'

'I don't know what he's saying, Mary, but that's what he's told me to do.'

'Well, we're not doing that! How dare he tell you to put a stamp on that and post it?' John didn't say anything, and Mary could see he was tired. 'John, it's Friday today,' she reasoned. 'That's going to be sitting in the post box all weekend. By the time it gets to North Riding Infirmary, it'll be Monday, then you'll be waiting another fortnight for an appointment to come through. No, we're not doing that. We're going to go down there and do what we're doing now. We're going to sit there at that hospital until we get an appointment, and then at least we're doing something.'

That was what they did, and, over the next couple of weeks, John had at least three appointments with different doctors, who told him that his problem was to do with either a nerve or a muscle behind the eye.

John was given an appointment to see a neurologist in six weeks, but, within a couple of days, he was vomiting violently. Mary called the doctor again. 'Something is happening to my husband,' she told him. 'We've been to see a specialist at North Riding hospital, who said that we were to call the doctor out if there was any change in his condition. Well, he's had three days of vomiting and can hardly hold himself up.'

'Okay, we'll stop that sickness,' the doctor assured Mary, relieving her for a moment before adding: 'I'll write a prescription out and it'll be ready for you to collect in a couple of hours.'

'Come down for it in a couple of hours?' Mary couldn't believe what she was hearing. 'Are you telling me you're not coming out to see him?'

'No. There is no need for me to come out to see him. Just come down and collect the prescription and that should sort him out.'

'How am I supposed to leave a man who's vomiting his head off when I'm the only one here to look after him? How am I supposed to leave him, and what if I didn't even have a car outside the front door – what then?'

'I'm sorry, Mrs Butterwick, that's all I can do.'

'I can't leave my husband the state he's in,' she pleaded. 'It's not good enough!'

'Do you want the prescription?'

'Yes,' she said sharply, realising that there was no way she was going to change his mind. 'Get writing it and I'll have to send someone down to fetch it, because I'm not leaving my husband in the state he's in. I've got a very sick man on my hands and I thought the least you could do would be to come and see him.'

The sickness pills didn't ease John's condition any, and it wasn't long before he was so weak that he couldn't stand to dress himself. The ambulance men were on strike and Mary couldn't see how she was going to hold John and put his clothes on at the same time, let alone walk him to the car. She picked up the phone. 'Carol?'

'What's up, Mum? You sound terrible.'

'Can you ask Tony to come over please, and help me dress your father?'

'Dress dad? Mum what are you on about?'

This was the first time Mary had told any of her children about John's illness, and it all came out in a flood.

'Don't worry. Tony will come down, he'll help you,' Carol reassured her.

Now she was waiting. Sitting on the bed her daughter had slept in as a teenager, while John lay in the next room. Where had the years gone? Carol was 30 now, with two young boys of her own. Mary didn't know when it was that she had started to recognise her children as adults and felt able to ask for their help. The reality of a switch in their relationship hit her now. More than anything, she needed Carol to play the grown-up, to be outwardly strong. Watching the snow fall, she prayed again: 'Please God, I'll do anything, just help me get John to hospital quickly.'

13

LOVE AND LOSS

Mary looked at the empty pillow beside her on the bed and wept. It was the first time she and John had been separated since the war years. It didn't feel right that she should be pushing her strong Black Watch soldier in a wheelchair. It felt even worse leaving him at the hospital, but, in her pain, she had to trust that it was for the best. It would only be for a short time, she was sure. The doctors would find out what was wrong, if it was a muscle or a nerve. They would care for him, make him well and he'd be home soon.

Every day, she asked 'What is the matter with my husband and what are you doing about it?', and each day she left with the same answers, which to her were no answer at all.

'We are doing tests, Mrs Butterwick,' or 'We are waiting for reports, Mrs Butterwick.'

There were other questions that needed answering too, like: 'Why did you let him fall?'

'Well, he has to have a shower, Mrs Butterwick.'

'Yes, I know that, but why didn't a nurse go in with him?'

In ten days, the staff filled out three accident forms for John, but Mary wasn't really asking how he had got the bruises; rather, she wanted to know why his injuries had been allowed to happen in the first place.

Eventually, she demanded that someone tell her what was going on: 'It's my national health rights to see a doctor,' she told the ward sister. 'I want a doctor to talk to me and tell me what you are doing to my husband.'

The next day, the phone rang. It was the ward sister.

'Will you be coming in for visiting hour today, Mrs Butterwick?'

'Of course I'm coming to visit him.'

'Well the doctor will see you after visiting today.'

At last, Mary thought. Hopefully she'd get some sense of the situation now.

That evening, when the designated visiting hour was up, Mary was asked to wait in a small side room, where the doctor would see her.

'When will John be coming home?' she asked, expectantly.

'Do you realise what is happening to your husband, Mrs Butterwick?' the doctor answered solemnly with a question of his own.

'Well, it's something to do with a muscle or a nerve in his eye, but no one can tell me which one. This has been going on for weeks now and he's not getting any better, which is why I've asked to see you.'

'Your husband has a brain tumour – he won't be going home.'

'What?' Mary couldn't believe what she was hearing.

'In a couple of days at the most he will be in a coma and unable to respond.'

'No, you're wrong!' she argued. 'Someone with a brain tumour is going mad and acting mad.'

'I'm sorry, but he has.'

Mary didn't understand. Just minutes before she had been talking to John about her day. He had known that his football team, Middlesbrough had played that day and was keen, as always, to know how they got on. As far as she was concerned, there was nothing wrong with his brain.

'You're the crazy one!' she laughed, hollowly. 'My husband is perfectly sane.'

The doctor stood silent. Mary started screaming. 'My husband's not mad! Come along with me to the ward and see for yourself!'

The next few hours passed by in a trance.

After hearing the seriousness of her father's condition, their youngest daughter, Julia, who was living in Hampton, Middlesex, secured her newborn daughter in the back of the car and drove home to Teesside to join the rest of the family. Mary embraced her daughter; there were too many feelings for words. As they walked down the long cold corridor, where Mary had wheeled John just days earlier, the ward sister stepped out of her room and called to them. 'Can I have a quick word, Mrs Butterwick?'

Mary and Julia stepped into the room, anxious not to waste the precious visiting time they had. Visitors were only allowed for one set hour a day, and twice at weekends.

'You can't do anything for your husband now. The best thing you can do is go home and forget him.'

Mary was dumbstruck. The nurse continued. 'I'm the only one who can help your husband now and, if you'll excuse me, I've got 30 other patients to look after.'

The sister left the room and Mary, without saying a word in response, began making towards the ward hurriedly. Suddenly realising Julia wasn't with her, she turned to find her daughter standing incredulous outside the office.

'Julia, what's the matter? Come on.'

'Mum, how could you allow that woman to speak to you like that?'

'What do you mean?'

'That woman in that office; speaking to you like that …'

'Julia, don't you realise – she doesn't matter?' Mary said softly. 'She doesn't matter to me. What matters to me is your father, and you've come to see him so let's go. He knows that you're here and that's what really matters.'

Julia was angry. 'Mum, if you can just let that go and let that woman speak to you like that, it's beyond me!'

'What?' Mary was tired of the fighting. 'It doesn't really matter. The most important thing is your father. He's waiting to say "Hello" to you.'

'But it's not "Hello" is it? Mum, after what she's told me and what you told me last night I can't go on that ward and just say "Goodbye" to my dad.'

'Of course you can,' Mary was adamant. 'Do it in any way you want to, Julia. The way you can see it in your heart – but right now that's all that matters.'

Julia looked at her mother, tears pricking her eyes. Mary took her hand. 'Let's go.'

The next day, John's condition had deteriorated further and he was unable to respond. Another doctor had reiterated the terrible news. For some time, John had been walking around with a primary tumour in his lung. The brain tumour was a secondary cancer. There was no way he was going to be coming home; there was no use in arguing any more.

After visiting ended, Mary called at the vicarage. When there was no reply, she ran desperately to the curate's house. 'John's worse. He's very, very ill and somebody has got to do something about it,' she pleaded.

'Come in,' he offered.

'Will you go and bless John, please? He can't receive anything, he's in a coma. He can't even talk to you, but perhaps if you went in and gave him a blessing … We've got to ask now because he is so ill.'

'Okay, come in and I'll call and ask if we can go now.'

Mary stepped in the house while the curate phoned the hospital.

'Ask if I can come with you,' she whispered.

He did, but the ward sister refused.

'I can go, but I'm sorry, you can't come with me,' he told her. 'Don't worry. Go home and I'll call you when I get back.'

Just over an hour after the curate had phoned Mary to say he had seen John, the hospital rang. Mary scraped the ice off the car frantically, but by the time she arrived her husband was dead.

14

AN ACHING CHASM

It was almost six months since John had died. Mary didn't want to use euphemisms – at least, not to kid herself. She hadn't 'lost' her husband; he had been taken from her. He was gone; dead; and the hole he'd left wasn't getting any smaller. Most days she wished she had died with him. What was left for her now? Her body sang no more.

It was the smallest of things she missed the most, like having someone with whom to share her tales from the day. Or her Saturday morning coffee in bed; of all things, why did she miss that so much?

There were so many unanswered questions. Why did no one tell her John was dying? Surely they must have known. Why did she not see it herself? Had he known and not told her? Why were they robbed of their last farewell? Why did they not have time to say 'I love you'? Why was there no compassion from the hospital staff? Why did they let him fall so many times? Why did they rob him of his dignity? Why did that sister tell her to go home and forget him? Maybe physically and medically she did care for John, but why couldn't she have been more careful with her words? Words can wound too. Why did the same sister refuse to let her in with the vicar when he went to give John a final blessing? Was a rule worth more than a life? She never saw John alive again after that – why did he die alone? Surely people should care for each other better than that.

'Where is the care, God?' she asked. 'I know I keep asking but I don't see it anywhere. Where are *you*, God? Where has the love gone?'

Mary tipped a bottle of tranquilisers into her hand. It would have been so easy to swallow them and end it all. End the never ending circle of unanswered questions, the constant pain that crushed her chest and the lonely life she no longer recognised.

Whether it was God or her own cowardice she couldn't work out, but something caused her to put the pills back in the bottle and soldier on.

She thought of her father and how she had hung over his coffin, sobbing, after everyone else had gone to bed. Pregnant at the time, she had nursed him for three months at home before he was taken into hospital where he died of a heart attack. Mary had been advised by the doctor to stay at home, something she didn't take kindly to. It meant that she didn't see her father again. After his death, the doctors advised that none of the family see the body. At the time, Mary didn't fully understand the reasons why, but she never let her real feelings show because her mother couldn't have coped with that. Only the dogs had seen her cry. She smiled, remembering the family's two white poodles, Sherry and Jingles, who provided the perfect excuse for her to escape and be on her own. They were such faithful companions, who never failed to sit patiently while she let out her tears on a quiet churchyard bench.

Following her father's death Mary nursed her mother through pleurisy, only to find that once her physical health began to improve her mental health deteriorated. She had often threatened to take her own life, dramatically claiming she would throw herself under a bus. Perhaps Mary was now going through the same.

John had always been there to support her. He was the gentle spirit, she was the restless one. She remembered the child she had miscarried at seven months. She had been stood at the kitchen table, baking for some friends who were visiting that evening. There didn't seem to be any reason for it – nothing out of the ordinary had happened that day – but suddenly she was bleeding. John called for the doctor but, by the time he arrived he had already delivered the baby himself. It was stillborn. Mary never saw her child; John shielded her from that. He only told her that it was a boy. That was John – always quiet and uncomplaining. Who would comfort her now?

Mary wondered if John had known he was ill and had tried to save her pain by not telling her. She knew that her brother, Jack, had done that, trying to shield everyone from his suffering.

Jack had died of flu during the 1968 pandemic. He was 32. Of course, the family knew he had always been weak, having only one working lung, but he hadn't told anyone that he had an abscess on the good one. The night before he died he told his mother that the doctors had suggested operating on his lungs, but he was against it. When she heard, Mary wrote a long letter, encouraging Jack to have the operation if that was what the doctors advised. She planned to give it to him in person the following day, but, just after 5am, she got a call from the hospital to say Jack had died. It fell to her to tell her mother, knowing it would collapse her world again.

She smiled to herself. Jack had not previously confided the seriousness of his condition to anyone except the bank manager.

'This brother of yours was one of the bravest men I've ever met,' he told her. 'He walked in here and made provisions for his wife, family and mother. He walked out of here knowing he was dying and took our advice.'

At the time, Jack had his own business. The bank's advice was to sell this and buy property so that he could leave a good home for his wife. He did so, taking a job as a door-to-door insurance salesman to earn a regular income. No doubt that job helped to kill him, Mary thought. If she closed her eyes, she could still see him, standing on her doorstep, soaked wet through with rain. He'd sit in the kitchen and joke with her while she served up a chip butty with a fried egg in it – his favourite. What she would give to open the door to him now – Jack and the collie dogs he always owned and loved – her baby brother, forever young. The tears came, until, exhausted, she slumped forward on the kitchen table and slept.

In the past, life had always seemed better after a sleep, but over these last few months Mary found it had brought no relief from the aching emptiness. She looked at the clock: half past three in the morning. There was no point in going to bed now. She would only toss and turn until she had to get up for work in a couple of hours.

As the kettle boiled, she looked out on the darkened street. There was only one other light on, in a house over the road. Another restless soul, she guessed. Although it was difficult to enjoy anything these days, she had grown to like the silence of the early hours.

Taking her tea into the sitting room, she flicked through the record collection she'd shared with John. It had been hard to listen to music since his death, because it could stir so much emotion that Mary didn't wish to unleash. She stopped; there it was: *Warsaw Concerto*. Oh, how that record used to take her to another world. It was the soundtrack to a romantic movie, *Dangerous Moonlight*, in which she'd lost herself several times at a darkened cinema. As a young girl, she would close her bedroom door and listen to it over and over, letting the sound of the piano sweep her into another realm. One day, her brother had sat on the record by accident, breaking it, and she had cried uncontrollably, worried that she would never have the money to buy another. Knowing how much she loved it, John had bought her this copy as a present. That fact made it even more special. She placed the needle gently on the record, settled in the armchair and closed her eyes.

It was so hard not to focus on what she didn't have, but Mary knew it was a choice – to choose life, to reject bitterness and to recognise her blessings. That didn't mean it was an easy choice, but it was a choice.

Her four children had given her tremendous strength to carry on, but she felt it unfair to lean unnecessarily on any one of them. They were all married and had families of their own to care for. Her grief was so all-encompassing that Mary felt she had nothing left to give them. They were in the prime of their lives – she needed to leave them to be free.

Scotland, that's where she would go. Maybe in the natural silence there she would begin to find some of the answers she so craved.

Kath welcomed Mary with a cheery smile, although she knew this wasn't to be an easy visit. The loss was written on every inch of Mary's body – how she held herself, how she spoke, the dullness in her eyes, how she listened sporadically. It was as if a light had been switched off inside her, and Kath didn't know how she could help to re-ignite it.

'Whatever you're feeling, Mary, it's okay,' she told her.

The pair hugged and Kath hoped that her love would somehow make it through the numbness to warm Mary's heart.

'Do you fancy a lobster for your tea?' she asked brightly.

Mary smiled, hesitantly. 'Kath, you don't have to go to any trouble for me.'

'It's no trouble.'

'How can you afford that? Really, I'm happy with a piece of toast and a cup of tea.'

'Don't be daft. You come all this way and think I'm going to serve up no more than a bit of bread. I thought you knew me better than that. Besides, I've a fisherman who owes me a favour and he'd be delighted to know I've called it in to help an old friend.'

Good to her word, by the end of the day there were two lobsters waiting on the doorstep. It seemed to Mary that Kath knew everyone and could get her hands on just about anything. This second fact was all the more remarkable because Kath never had a bean to her name, but got by on the philosophy that one good turn deserves another. If a local fisherman or grocer needed a lift somewhere she'd take him, then when she needed an edible treat, he'd return the favour.

'You have to get paid in kind, Mary,' she explained, when Mary questioned why she'd been working at the same garage for almost 30 years without a wage. 'He'd do me a favour if I needed it, so I did him a favour when he hit on hard times. As long as I've got enough money for a loaf of bread and a packet of fags, I'm happy.'

For Kath, life wasn't about what you had in a material sense; the important thing was how you treated other people and how they treated you. Being around her was just the tonic Mary needed. It was going to be a slow process, but her crushed spirit was beginning to feel restored.

During the day, Mary would wander along the coast for miles, without seeing a single person. Watching and listening to the gentle movement of the waves stretching all the way to the horizon calmed her. Here she felt that there was nothing between her and God, and there was so much she wanted to ask him, so much anger she needed to dispel. Why John? Why this way? Where is the care, where is the love, where are you, God? Where are you in all of this mess?

Sometimes it is okay to have no answers, to have no explanations, nor even any words. Kath knew that, even if at the time Mary didn't, and she was there for her friend with what she could provide – the unspoken, understated love and care that Mary desperately needed.

15

RETURNING TO THE WORLD

Back in Stockton, while Mary still had her part-time job working in a tea factory, she found it difficult to settle back into any type of routine.

'All this tea – who is drinking it?' she wondered, watching hundreds upon hundreds of tea bags drop into cardboard boxes before being sealed in cellophane on their journey down the conveyor belt, and off to kitchen cupboards who knows where.

Tea was the great English comforter, although at this end of the process it seemed nothing but an irritant. It was to Mary right now, anyway. There was something hypnotic about the never-ending loop of the conveyor belt; at least, she hoped it would be never ending as it was her job to teach staff how to use these huge machines and keep them running. Yet, when she shook herself from the trance, everything there seemed pointless to her now. 'What am I doing here? If I don't do something else I shall go mad.'

She remembered first taking the job. It was to help pay for Keith to go on a canoeing holiday with the school. That was 12 years ago, and she was still there. It all seemed so long ago – another lifetime.

The golden rule in the Butterwick house was always that if one child got something then the others got the same, or something of equivalent value. So, when Keith came asking for £40 for a holiday, there was no way they could afford it.

'Let's sit down and talk about this, Keith,' Mary had reasoned. 'If your father and I give you that, it means that all four of you have got to get the same.'

Keith looked deflated. He'd set his sights on this trip. It was his last year at school and, as he saw it, he'd never get another chance to do anything so exciting with his friends.

'I'm not saying you can't go.' His face lit up at her words. 'Wait for it,' she added quickly. 'It just means that you're going to have to work for this holiday, as I am.'

'What does that mean?' he looked puzzled.

'Okay. I'll make this bargain with you. If you get a part-time job after school, I'll do the same, and for every £1 you put away towards the holiday, I'll put away two.'

'Thanks, mum, that's brilliant!' he beamed. Of course, he didn't know quite what he'd let himself in for.

Keith got a job working as an errand boy at a local dairy, delivering butter and groceries on his bike, while Mary took a job at a tea factory nearby. How her heart would ache to see him collect his heavy, cast iron bicycle and ride off in all weathers to fetch and carry his orders.

'I have to stop this,' she told John, grabbing the bike. 'I can't bear to face my kid riding this bicycle any more. I want to do it for him.'

'You've got to stop that,' he replied, matter of fact.

'I'm going to tell him tonight – he'll have to give his notice in because I can't cope with it any longer.'

'Don't you dare do that!' John was adamant. 'It'll only cause trouble. The boy needs to learn the value of money and he's not complaining. He'll enjoy the holiday all the more knowing how much he's earned it.'

And so it was. All through the winter, hail and snow, Keith rode out on his bike and, although it pained her to watch him, Mary didn't say a word.

In hindsight now, she could see that John was right. He had a knack of cutting through emotions to the real quick of the matter – which could annoy the hell out of her. Fresh air never harmed anyone. If only she had recognised the risks of her own employment.

Of course there were the obvious dangers from the machinery; you could easily lose a finger, or, indeed, a hand, in some of the equipment. As an instructor, there were many trainees she had to fail because they didn't meet the grade on safety. It was for their own good, but knowing that it could mean they couldn't work meant Mary still hated having to do it.

Now staff wore protective clothing, including masks, but Mary had worked there for more than a decade without such precautions. No doubt, she believed, this contributed to her emphysema, although there was doubt, of course, because the company had never accepted any link between working conditions and chest problems, for her or any of the staff. It was just how things were back then, no-one thought about health and safety in the way they did today.

Mary hadn't even been concerned when the hospital called her back for further X-rays. She supposed the first must have just been a bad picture, that's all, but John insisted on taking the day off and going with her.

'So, what do you think is the problem, Mr Harrison?' she asked.

The consultant got up from his desk to meet her. 'I'm just so amazed at you.'

'What do you mean? What's wrong with me?'

'Well, Mrs Butterwick, according to the pictures I've seen of your lungs, I expected you to walk into this office with two sticks. I'm absolutely amazed.'

'Well, thank goodness I'm like this,' she laughed.

It was only when she came out of the office that she realised how concerned John looked.

'What's up with you? You look terrible.'

'I feel terrible.'

'Why – what do you feel so terrible about?'

'I know you weren't worried, and I didn't have the heart to say anything to you, but I thought we were going to go in there to hear you had cancer of the lung or something.'

'Honestly!' Mary was surprised; the thought of it being something serious had never even crossed her mind.

'Yes – that doctor was shocked. He expected to see you as a vastly different person.'

'And, as I told him, thank goodness I'm as I am, eh? Now come on.'

She shook her head at the memory of it all. 'Oh, John – to think you were the one worried about me.'

'Is life ever as it seems?' she wondered. The loss of John had taught her that nothing could be taken for granted. It was time for a change; to do something else with her life, of that she was certain.

Part 3

DREAMING OF A BETTER WORLD

16

LEARNING TO LAUGH AGAIN

The seeds of Butterwick Hospice were already sown in Mary's heart but, at this point, even she couldn't envisage what was to come. All she knew was that she wanted to put back into the world some of the care she felt was lacking. She also knew that if she didn't do something useful with her time that she was in danger of going stir crazy.

What was she going to do? That was a whole other question. 'But,' she thought, 'one step at a time.' Mary trusted that something would turn up and, sure enough, that week in the parish magazine she noticed a small advertisement for volunteers to help out at services held at the hospital chapel.

Making the first call to the chapel was the hardest. Mary was nervous. What if whoever answered didn't need her, or, worse still, decided they didn't want her help? Could she even be of any help to anyone else in her current state? She wasn't certain. Nevertheless, she picked up the phone and, to her relief, the person at the other end sounded delighted to hear from her. Before she knew it, Mary had agreed to help out that coming weekend.

At first, it was simply a case of going into the hospital on a Sunday morning and helping patients get to the service, either by providing a supporting arm to walk with them from the ward to the chapel, or pushing those less mobile in a wheelchair.

After a few weeks, Mary began to think: 'I really like working here.' It was a surprise. She knew that she needed to get out of the house and do something useful, but she hadn't expected to enjoy it. So, when the chaplain asked if anyone would be able to spare a couple of hours in the week to go onto the wards with him, Mary jumped at it.

'You know, voluntary services are crying out for people like you,' he told her. 'I'll give you the number and, if you do find you have some time you could offer, I know they would bite your hand off.'

Mary's early morning shift at the tea factory finished at lunchtime, so, the next afternoon, she took the number out of her purse and dialled.

'Hello, I've been given your number by a friend who said that you might be looking for people to help out,' she enquired, tentatively.

The voice came back in a matter of fact manner that, while not unpleasant, felt to Mary a little abrupt. 'What have you got to offer?'

'Well,' she hesitated a little. 'I've got a car, a telephone and every afternoon of the week if you want it.'

Mary heard an audible gasp at the other end. She was invited to start the very next day.

One of her first tasks was to collect Margaret, a young woman who had cerebral palsy, and take her to a weekly group for those with disabilities held in an old school building, which was now a community centre. Being her first time, Mary was a little nervous about what was expected of her. She helped Margaret into the centre and, spying a woman who looked like she could be in charge, Mary enquired gently: 'Excuse me, I've just brought someone here, but I'm not sure what to do now. Do I wait and take her home, or will someone else do that?'

The woman answered quickly, without much attention. 'Please yourself, you can either go home or you can stop and make yourself useful. It's up to you!'

'Crikey,' Mary thought, 'we've got a right one here!' Still, she didn't really have anything better to do so she thought she might as well stay and see what it was all about.

'Don't mind Mrs Fordham,' one of the volunteers, Reg, smiled. 'Her bark's worse than her bite. If you ever get beyond the sergeant major exterior you'll find a heart of gold.'

Mary tried to relax, and made herself busy running from room to room with cups of tea. She went back the next week and it wasn't long before she found herself actually looking forward to going. She was learning to laugh again. The experience had renewed her sense of fun and she found herself trying to make people laugh, wanting to see them smile.

Noticing her cheerful spirit, Val, another volunteer, commented one evening: 'I can't get over you, Mary.'

'What do you mean?' Mary asked, puzzled.

'Well, someone told me you recently lost your husband and yet here you are helping out, giving so much of yourself. I don't know how you are coping, but what you do here is amazing, it really is.'

Val lived across the road from the school where the group was held, and invited Mary into her home for a coffee. Mary welcomed the chance to explain what being part of the group meant to her, but once she started talking it was like she couldn't stop. She found herself opening up to Val, telling of the hurt and anger that was still inside her about the way John was treated at the end of his life. Suddenly, Mary noticed that it had gotten very dark outside. 'Dear me, is that the time? I'd better be going.'

Val looked at her watch. Mary had been talking for three hours solid. 'Let me make us a cup of tea first – you've a long drive home,' Val smiled. She had begun to realise the depth of Mary's grief and her admiration and friendship grew with this understanding.

Although Mary's hurt was never far from the surface, being part of a group and feeling she was making a contribution was touching her heart. If someone didn't show up for a couple of weeks in a row, she started asking why. Why were people who loved coming to the group not showing up any more?

Not wanting to appear as if she was taking over, she tentatively suggested: 'I was thinking, Mrs Fordham – seeing as how I take the register, if someone isn't here for three weeks, would you mind if I gave them a call to see how they are doing?'

Without a second thought, Mrs Fordham replied: 'If that's what you want to do, you do it.'

For Mary, it was all about connecting with people and showing care in a practical way. Yes, she was there to help out for a couple of hours a week, but she wanted the friends she made there to know that she cared about their lives outside the group too.

However, when Reg didn't show up for a couple of weeks she was a little hesitant to call. They had become good friends in the group, but Reg was a private man and she knew little of his life other than that he was a widower and lived alone. She eventually tried calling him a couple of times with no luck. She didn't want to intrude, but, after three weeks of meetings with no Reg, she started to become more concerned.

'Hello,' the voice at the other end of the phone sounded frail and uncertain.

'Reg, is that you?' she asked.

'Yes – who's this?'

'Oh, thank goodness. It's Mary, Mary Butterwick from the disabled group.'

'Hello, Mary,' his voice lifted as he spoke, and Mary felt that she could hear him smile. He told her that he'd been in hospital for an operation, and Mary asked whether, if he couldn't make it to the group the following week, he would mind if she dropped in for a cup of tea.

It never ceased to amaze Mary what talents people had hidden away. Reg's home was full of the most wonderful handmade furniture.

'That's a lovely corner cupboard,' she remarked, looking around the room.

'I made that,' he said.

Mary stood up to examine the carving; it was beautiful. 'Is this what you do for a living?'

'No, it's just a hobby,' he said modestly. 'Keeps me busy.'

'I'll say. I can't believe it, Reg – people would pay a fortune for furniture like this.'

'Oh, I don't know about that,' he smiled, embarrassed. 'It's just something I do in my spare time. It makes me happy.'

Mary only visited his home three or four times before Reg was fit enough to come back to the group and volunteer, but in that time their friendship deepened and, on his request, Mary took Reg along to her church, where he later met his second wife.

Soon, the long, lonely hours which had so haunted Mary were becoming ever shorter. In fact, she was starting to feel that there weren't enough hours in the day to do everything she'd like. So much so that she sometimes questioned: 'Am I running *from* life, or *into* real life?'

So often, people would say: 'I don't know how you do that, Mary.'

'Do what?'

'Work with those sick and disabled people all the time.'

'Come off it,' she'd laugh. 'They do much more to help me than I ever do to help them. These people keep me going, why do you think I keep coming back?'

It was true. Mary didn't see a disability or an illness, she saw a person. The illness and disability was only one small part, but it was the part which allowed her to give to them what she felt she had been denied herself – care and love when she most needed it. It was this that made life worth living again. Whatever it was, and she tried not to question it too much, it was making her feel alive – something she hadn't felt for a long time.

As well as her work with the community group for the disabled, she found herself becoming more and more involved at the hospital. Yet, no matter how many times she saw patients being treated in what she considered an undignified way, it still grieved her, re-igniting the fire of injustice that was still burning from John's death. Often, she would see patients left waiting in corridors, their bodies marked out for treatment where everyone passing could see, and yet they'd been told very little about what was happening to them. Time and again, Mary asked herself: 'Where is the dignity and respect? How must these people feel, how are they coping?'

She trained as a bereavement counsellor, and became instrumental in bringing Cruse Bereavement Care to the area as well as working with another group, Coping with Cancer, which offered support to those who had received a cancer diagnosis and their families. To her horror, Mary found that many people who had been diagnosed with cancer weren't being offered any treatment. To her, it seemed as if the consultants had given up hope already. She saw people in desperate need of someone to talk to – people who felt completely abandoned by the medical profession because they had been given a devastating prognosis and then told not to come back for three months.

'What is this word, "terminal"?' Mary would ask, much to doctors' irritation. They knew exactly what it meant in a medical sense, but explaining it to the lay person was something else, and they really didn't feel they had the time, nor the necessity, to do so. When Mary discovered that 'terminal' didn't necessarily mean a person was going to die imminently, it changed her whole outlook on how she viewed the diagnosis. Put simply, it just meant that there was no known cure, so the doctors weren't trying to cure the person any more. 'You can't sit back and accept this,' she'd often advise patients. 'You've got to fight – to go back to the consultant and tell them that you want something done.'

Very often, those same patients, after questioning their lack of treatment, would then be offered some medical help. Like Clare, who, after having her second child by caesarean section was told that the doctors had detected cancer in her body, for which there was no treatment. After a few weeks of counselling Clare, Mary insisted that she get some treatment, and that she would support her in asking for it. Knowing that she was not alone restored a positive focus to Clare's otherwise crumbling world. Despite being told initially to go home to die, Clare received treatment and lived for another seven years – long enough to see her son into junior school; long enough for him to know and love his mother.

17

A VISION OF LOVE

Mary was becoming a great listener for all around her, but she rarely unburdened her troubles on anyone. It was more than a year since John's death. After such a time she imagined that people would think she should be over it. Sometimes she thought she should be too, although at the same time she doubted that she ever would be. Not that there was much time to dwell on it any more.

By helping others Mary had begun to recognise how selfish she had become in her grief. How easy it would be, even now, to be sucked down into the despair of it and never come back up. But the voluntary work had given her a new routine and purpose. She couldn't allow herself to focus on the hole inside, although, just because she spoke of it less, it didn't mean it had disappeared.

On Sunday morning, when Mary arrived at the hospital chaplaincy, the regular chaplain was away and there was a new vicar standing in at the service. Mary hadn't met him before, but when they got chatting afterwards it emerged that she knew his parish, St John the Baptist, well.

'Years ago I was a Sunday school teacher there, and it was my parish as a young girl,' she told him, smiling as the fond memories came to the fore. Mary had spent so much time there while growing up. Her mother was part of the Mothers' Union and she'd often take Mary along to help out making tea at the meetings. That church building had since been demolished, but, now he mentioned it, she found she could still see it clearly in her mind's eye. The church had been such a large part of her early social life. Well, there had been little else in terms of entertainment, not that the family could afford anyway. That said, Mary never felt deprived because there had always been lots of fun to be had with the parish badminton club and church garden parties.

'You might be interested in a framed picture we've had done to mark the parish's centenary,' the chaplain suggested. 'It's of the old church, the one you would know.'

'Yes, I wouldn't mind one of those for old times' sake,' she said politely. 'How much are they?'

'They are £50 with the frame. Call at the vicarage sometime and I'll show you.'

'£50!' Mary was taken aback by the expense. She thought it sounded a bit over the top for what they were selling and, although she didn't say it out loud, her face must have said it all.

'We've got them unframed as well,' he added. 'Come and have a look, and if you don't buy one, that's fine.'

A couple of days later Mary called at the vicarage. The pictures on sale were prints of a drawing of the old church, where it used to stand by the gas works.

'I'll pay you the £50, but I don't like the frame. It's not my idea of a frame,' she told him straight.

The vicar laughed. Mary didn't want the picture. She was only buying it as a donation to the parish centenary fund, and he knew that. 'Here, read this,' he said, taking a book from the shelf and handing it to her.

'What is it?' she asked surprised.

'Has nobody ever told you that you are in grief? Read that and I promise you, you won't stop reading it until you've finished.'

Mary looked at the little book in her hand, C. S. Lewis's *A Grief Observed*, then raised her eyes slowly to meet the vicar's. No one had ever said to her before that she was in grief. After the words were spoken it seemed obvious really, yet hearing it said out loud changed everything, allowing her to see it for herself. It was a welcome acknowledgement of the pain she still felt but couldn't speak of. This vicar whom she barely knew was giving her permission to grieve, and the feeling was overwhelming. Mary could only say: 'Thank you.'

That night she started reading the book, and the rawness of C. S. Lewis's own grief for his wife jumped from the pages. Here was a man who knew the same pain as her, someone she could relate to; she was not alone any more.

A couple of days later, Mary returned the book. The vicar wasn't in so she pushed it through the door with a note to say:

You were absolutely right, I couldn't put it down. But I didn't just read it once – I read it half a dozen times. Thank you.

Mary had thought her grief so large, so all-encompassing, that no one could understand the depth of her pain, and, as such, no one could reach out and soothe it. Now she began to understand just how many people shared her pain, not just for John, but for so many people loved and lost.

For the first time, she was able to see that John was in a better place now – he was with God. It wasn't for John that she was crying; it was for herself. When she said that she wanted John back, she wanted him back as he had been, fit and well before his illness. His death had changed her life forever; she could never be the same person again, but she was still here so what did that mean? How would she be now? How *could* she be now?

That following Sunday, after the service, Mary was full of questions for the vicar – questions about death, dying and the afterlife. Questions most people find themselves asking at some point; questions that have been asked forever and never truly answered.

'Do you read the Bible, Mary?' the vicar asked, answering her with a question of his own.

Mary did have a Bible. She'd won it as a prize, aged 12, for coming top of the class in needlework. It was treasured, but rarely read.

'I do, but it's all "thee" and "thou" – I can't make head nor tail of it,' she told him.

'Why don't you get a modern version, and you'll understand it better,' he suggested.

He'd certainly been right about the last book he recommended, and, as all her questions were really directed at God, perhaps he was right about this one too. She still had the £5 her mother had given her on her birthday. She'd been saving it to buy a special gift, but now she knew what that would be.

Each lunch time, when she got home from the factory, after removing her clothes and showering until the water ran clear of the tea dust that infused itself in every pore, Mary would sit at the table with a cup of coffee in one hand and a bacon sandwich in the other, and read.

'Lord, I'm so thick, I need things knocking into me to see them,' she prayed. 'Please open my eyes and spirit to give me whatever I need to take from this reading.'

Each day she said that short prayer before her reading, and each day her faith grew. Mary had always attended church and so had heard these stories many times, yet now they seemed clearer. If before she knew them in her head, now she felt them in her heart.

That said, she still had lots of questions, but she didn't think God would mind her asking them. After all, how else was she to learn? Mary didn't always find the answers she thought she was seeking. Sometimes she only found more questions, but in her searching she had opened up a conversation with God.

Jesus said: 'Come to me, all of you who are tired and have heavy loads, and I will give you rest.' Well, here *she* was admitting that she didn't have it all together; she was still hurting – she had serious, deep wounds that she didn't know how to care for. She was crying out for help and asking God to heal her.

When Mary was a young woman in the army, she always believed that someone or something was looking out for her. She used to call it her good fairy and there were many strokes of good luck and coincidence she had put down to its presence. Now she saw and felt that presence as the Holy Spirit, whom she was inviting to guide her, allowing her soul to listen, her heart to open and her spirit to grow.

On the outside, nothing had changed, but on the inside Mary began to feel an overwhelming sense of love that both calmed and invigorated her. It was as if she was seeing the world afresh and she wanted so much to do something for God, although what that was she didn't yet know.

She didn't feel alone or frightened any more. Of course she still missed John, but death, she was coming to accept, was a part of life which came to everyone eventually. It still upset her to think of John dying alone, without the opportunity to say a final goodbye, but now she saw his death not as a goodbye but simply a farewell. To accept this, she had to open her heart and forgive. She had to learn to hand her troubles over to God and trust that he would handle them.

This all sounded good, but it wasn't going to be easy. If she was to move on, she needed to forgive the medical staff who made careless comments, especially the sister on the ward where John died, and she needed to forgive herself. She had tortured herself with 'what if?'s Perhaps she should have known better, and not accepted so quickly that John's condition was due to a problem with a muscle or a nerve behind the eye as the doctors had initially suggested. Should *she* have been able to see that he had cancer?

Looking back, when Julia had her first baby on New Year's Eve, Mary had desperately wanted to go and visit her. She pleaded with John to drive down but he wouldn't. Mary couldn't understand this because he'd always driven all over the country before. Why didn't he want to see his own daughter and new grandchild? In the end he was determined not to take the car so they went by train. Perhaps she should have realised then that there was something amiss, but nothing told her anything was seriously wrong.

Facing these doubts was like staring into a huge pile of regrets which had to be worked through. Sometimes it was hard for her to even like herself, let alone to forgive. Carrying all this stuff around was a miserable existence.

However, forgiving and forgetting are two very different things. What Mary could never forget was the unnecessary pain caused to John by neglect, be it intentional or not. She could not accept the inability of some people to treat others as human beings, and that meant everyone, even those who had been diagnosed as being terminally ill. Whatever that meant in real terms, and she still didn't fully understand it, she knew it didn't mean that these people were any less alive than any one else.

The important part, in her eyes, was to get on with living and to make the most of opportunities. To care for one another and to let those closest to us know how much we love and value them – simple things, which cost so little in monetary terms, but which can mean so much. It was these simple things which she felt had been denied to John at the end; so much had been left unsaid, so much anger uncalmed.

She remembered standing at her bedroom window when John was ill and pleading with God, saying that she'd do anything if only he would bring them help. She knew you weren't supposed to bargain with God, but maybe that's what she did that day. She said she'd do anything, but what anything was she didn't yet know. Whatever it was, she vowed to do what she could and trust God to do what she couldn't.

Mary realised that whenever she felt there was nothing she could do, that of course there was. She could pray. 'If only we prayed more, for each other, for the normal everyday needs of life, we could change the world,' she thought.

One day, after her prayer time, she began writing. She often found writing therapeutic, a way to get her thoughts together and make sense of the noise in her head. This day, however, the words weren't about how she could help a particular patient or work her time better. Instead, she found herself writing about a house. No, it wasn't just a house, this was a *home*.

It was a large home; light and airy. Its space gave a sense of freedom, to be whoever you wanted, to share laughter or find solitude. At the same time, although it was big, it was also cosy. There was a glowing fire burning downstairs, thick-piled carpet underfoot, soft fluffy towels and crisp bed linen. There was attention to detail in the paintings on the walls and the fresh flowers in vases on tables and window ledges. Everything in the home shared the same purpose: to make it a welcoming place where people felt safe and instantly comfortable.

Mary read back what she had just written. She didn't just want this to be an imaginary place. This house was real. This was the place that she had been so in need of when John took ill. This was the place that would provide everything she had been denied at that time. She began writing, frantically now: it was a place where people were treated as individuals, where each life mattered, where each thought mattered, where care and love mattered. It was a place where people could come to be renewed when life was hard. Where, even if they couldn't be made physically better, they could spend some time and leave feeling healthier in mind and spirit. It was an uplifting place, where people would visit for a day, or even just half a day. They would eat wholesome, home-made food, having a little bit of what they fancied when they fancied it. If they wanted to read, they could read; if they wanted to chat, they could chat; if they wanted to play dominoes, let them play dominoes. Care and companionship were the only rules of this house.

That said, if this house was going to offer care and support to the terminally ill, then she supposed that it would need a doctor, or at least a nurse. Someone who knew what they were doing in terms of medicine. Yet, for every medic, it would need at least 20 other people – caring people who could help with other things, important things that so easily got overlooked in times of ill health, like help with finances, help with cleaning and shopping and arranging days out. It sounded like an idyllic place, but, as she let her imagination run, Mary never fooled herself that this would be an alternative to hospital. It wasn't a place to come to *cure* the body of illness and disease, although, if that happened, all well and good. For all those whom the hospital had dismissed as beyond help, it would restore hope, celebrate life and, even if it couldn't heal the body, it would do its best to heal the heart and soul.

18

MAKING DREAMS HAPPEN

Mary couldn't get the idea of this wonderful home out of her mind. She went to sleep thinking about it, and it was the first thing she thought of when she awoke.

She had to tell someone, but who would listen? The doctors at the hospital all thought she was mad. Even her vicar, who she'd always found so compassionate in the past, had begun to think her crazy in grief. Could she blame them, really? Here was she, a middle-aged woman, with no formal education and little money to her name, who was questioning everything and, worse still, thought she might have the answers to right what she saw as the wrongs of the world. When put that way, she could see their point. So, rather than risk ridicule straight away, she decided to share her idea with two close friends, Monica and Jo.

Afternoon tea was an English tradition Mary savoured, and she loved to do it properly, with china cups, cake and scones. She always made sure to pour the milk first and then the tea. It had been some weeks since she and her friends had had an opportunity to relax together in this way, and there was a lot to catch up on. Monica told how her daughter was expecting her third grandchild, and Jo entertained them with tales of her mischievous new puppy. Then it was Mary's turn.

'So, Mary, what's this news you needed to tell us?' asked Monica.

Mary could contain her excitement no longer. She reached into the drawer and took out the paper on which she'd scribbled frantically.

'What's this?' Jo laughed. 'I think you need a few handwriting lessons, Mary.'

'Don't be cheeky,' she hit back playfully. 'Just read it and tell me what you think.'

'Here, give it to me, I'll read it,' said Monica, taking the paper from Jo's hands. She began to read it out loud and, as she spoke, Mary felt warmth inside. It was as if, just by speaking it, Monica was helping to bring her dream to life.

Monica put the paper down. 'So, what do you think?' Mary asked, impatient in her excitement to hear their views.

'If this is a real place and it's going to happen, then it will happen,' said Monica in her own philosophical way.

'I just know something is going to happen,' said Mary, enthused. 'I just don't know how or when!'

Jo was suddenly serious. 'The community needs this, Mary. I believe it *will* happen. It will happen like stepping stones, and, like stepping stones, you've just got to walk across them.'

Several months later, the three friends were invited, through their voluntary work at the hospital, to meet the Sister-in-charge of palliative care at St Thomas' Hospital in London. The visit involved a tour of the wards, talking about some of the latest mattresses and equipment used to make patients more comfortable, after which they finished up in the Sister's office for tea.

'Thank you so much for seeing us, Sister,' Monica said. 'I'm sure we've taken up quite enough of your time, but before we go, is there anything else you can think of that we could do to help terminally ill patients back home?'

'I can't think of anything,' she smiled. Then, just as the others began to get up to leave, she added: 'Oh, I almost forgot – the day care.'

'What's that?' Mary asked.

'Oh, it's the greatest of blessings already and it's only been opened a few months, if that,' the Sister explained. 'It's the brain child of one of our surgeons. It's the first of its kind in the country.' As the sister continued, the three friends looked at each other in wonder. This was the type of place that Mary had written about, yet how could she have known? Indeed, she didn't know about this place. If other people elsewhere in the country had begun to feel the same, then obviously there was an even greater need for this type of house than they could have imagined.

Very soon afterwards, Mary arranged a visit to this new day care centre in Christchurch, in Dorset. She could hardly believe such a place really existed, and felt that she needed proof, in the form of photographs or a film, to convince others back home that they could build something similar.

Carol and Tony were the only ones she knew with such technology at that time, but when she asked to borrow it, Tony laughed. 'You'll never be able to use it properly,' he said. Mary was silent but disheartened, until he quickly added: 'I'll come with you and film it for you – otherwise it will be a waste of time.' Mary was thrilled, and the two of them drove down to be greeted by the centre's founder, Charles Hall, who had spent five years raising the £75,000 necessary to get the project off the ground.

Charles introduced them to patients, volunteers and staff. Mary chatted to everyone, while Tony followed behind with the heavy camera balanced on his shoulder – he'd been right, she never could have carried it herself, never mind got it to focus on anything useful! The visit filled Mary with encouragement, yet, back in the car, she couldn't stop the tears from flowing. Tears for all those who hadn't had, and would never experience, such care at the end of their lives, and more tears because she had no clue how she was ever going to find £75,000 to bring the same care to Teesside.

The reality of the cost involved had come as a blow to Mary. She'd always been brought up to believe that love and care were free, but all the good grace in the world wasn't going to magic up £75,000. Still, crying about it wasn't helping anyone. If £75,000 was what it was going to take, then she would have to find the money. How, she didn't know, but, as Jo had said, this project would be achieved through stepping stones. The fact that she'd seen it was possible elsewhere had just confirmed this; now she had to take the next step, and trust there would be another stone to catch her.

Once home, Mary sat down at her kitchen table, opened her notebook and tried to work out financially how this could be done.

Asking other people for money was out of the question. She felt she'd already become known as 'the crazy woman in grief', and was aware that doctors would quickly change direction or hide if they saw her coming. No, she would have to think of a way to get it started herself; she would have to prove that what she was saying could work, was *going* to work. It would take a long time, she knew that, but only then, with the foundations already in place, could she expect to be taken seriously.

Was this the best thing to do? Was this the right thing to do? There were no easy answers; every question seemed to lead to another question. To continue asking the big questions, for which she had no answers, was only weakening her resolve. It was the surest way to do nothing. So she plodded on, trusting that the answers would come to her eventually and, even if she couldn't see the end of the path, at least she'd see the next stepping stone, which was all she needed for now.

Maybe she didn't yet have as much money as it seemed that she needed, but she did have some money with which to get started. Could she run a centre from her own home? No, that wouldn't work because it wasn't that kind of house; but what kind of house was it? What if she sold her house to free up some money, and bought a smaller one to live in? What if she tried to borrow or get a second mortgage? If she did sell her house, she would still need somewhere to live; she couldn't become a burden to her family in that sense – even if they would let her, she wouldn't allow that to happen. If anything, she would need to buy something larger than the dorma bungalow in which she now lived. It wasn't just the money, either. What was this going to cost her emotionally? If she was going to sell her home, she guessed she had better tell her children first. This wasn't just her life she was changing; taking this step would mean the children would lose their inheritance. She had to make that clear to them and get their blessing, because she knew that once she set off on this path there was no turning back.

'You must do as you feel right, Mum,' Keith told her. Thankfully, all of her children told her the same in their own way and, shortly after, her bungalow was put up for sale.

19

A LEAP OF FAITH

Mary had started her journey and, having decided the path she was taking, she wanted to tell anyone who would listen about her plans. The idea was so exciting that she found herself sitting up with friends until four and five o'clock in the morning, outlining how she saw this house and what benefits it would bring to the community.

After scouring every estate agent in the area, she set her sights upon 10 Hartburn Lane, a three-storey Victorian semi in Stockton. In her dreams, she could see it operating just as she had imagined. She saw the pictures on the walls, the flowers on the window ledge, the patients coming in and the caring staff. The place was filled with smiling faces and laughter. Yes, this was the house that she would make into a home.

She swiftly put in an offer of £19,000, only to be disappointed when it was refused with derision. It was £2,000 short of the asking price, but it was the price she could afford and, as difficult as it was to admit it, she could not go any higher.

As the months went by, it became harder for Mary to maintain her initial enthusiasm. Perhaps she shouldn't have been telling anyone about her project at all, at least until there was something solid to tell. Having her offer turned down on 10 Hartburn Lane was only part of the problem – she had also not anticipated just how long it might take to sell her bungalow. Not only had she not had any offers, she hadn't had a single viewer. 'Am I doing the right thing after all?' she wondered.

It wasn't long before she was due to go on holiday with the group for the disabled. She had been looking forward to it, but something inside told her not to go – it wasn't the right time, not now. She called Monica.

'Monica, I'm not coming next week,' she said.

'What do you mean, you're not coming?' Monica couldn't believe what she was hearing.

'I don't know why, I just don't want to go.'

'But you've paid now, and you've roped us into going with you! You can't mean this?'

'I know it sounds crazy, and I realise I'll have to lose the money, but I can't, really.'

'And that's it? Are you ill or something?'

'No, I'm not ill.'

'You're just feeling fed up because you haven't sold that house of yours yet. You can't do everything yesterday you know, Mary.'

'I'm sorry, Monica, I won't change my mind. I'm not trying to make it difficult for you, but I can't go.'

A week later, Mary stood on the pavement, tears streaming down her face, as she waved the group off on their trip.

'What are you doing here, Mary?' Monica asked, bewildered. 'You should be on that coach with us, you big softy! There is only one person stopping you from coming and having a good time, and that's you.'

Returning home, Mary hung her anorak on the hook by the door, and filled the kettle. 'You and your blooming instincts,' she thought, catching a glimpse of her tear-stained face in the mirror. Just as she was sitting down with her coffee, the phone rang. 'Mrs Butterwick?' It was the estate agent. 'I've got a man here who wants to come and have a look at your bungalow.'

'When?'

'Now.'

'What – you mean, right now?'

Mary dashed around, tidying quickly where she could. Ten minutes later the door bell rang and, within half an hour, the place was sold.

'Don't you want to look at the garage and the garden?' she asked.

'No, I've seen around the bungalow, that's good enough for me. That's it – I'll buy it.'

'But you've only been here 15 minutes.'

'Do you want to sell it or don't you? I don't want any messing about: it'll be a cash sale – no solicitors wasting time.'

Mary was open-mouthed. After weeks of waiting, it was all happening so quickly. Thank goodness she'd not gone on that holiday! Coincidence seemed to be following her around these days, or perhaps she was being taught to listen to her heart more – to trust her spirit and know that, even if she couldn't see how, things would work out for the best.

Shortly after, the estate agent rang to confirm what the buyer had told her. Yes, the viewer was putting in an offer, it would be a cash sale for the full asking price and would she accept it? Mary had to pinch herself; surely this was a dream?

On the following Monday morning, the door bell rang. It was the buyer; 'Maybe he's come to his senses and decides he wants a more detailed look around,' thought Mary.

'I just thought I'd better tell you that I want to be in within two weeks,' he stated confidently.

Mary didn't know what to say. 'Do you want to come in?' she offered.

'No, just want to make sure you'll leave all the amenities – electricity and so on – turned on. None of it should be a problem. Since it's a cash sale and there are no solicitors involved, we should get all of this sorted within the fortnight.

'Oh, right,' Mary said, stunned.

'Okay – that's sorted then. You'll better get packing,' he said, heading down the path, and, just before he got in the car, he turned and shouted: 'Don't forget – get those tea chests out! You've got two weeks!'

Mary shut the door in a daze. It hadn't been a dream. This was really happening, but what now? In two weeks, she would have no home. Perhaps fortunately, she didn't have too much time to dwell on that fact. As the man said, she'd better start packing.

On hearing of her mother's imminent circumstances, Carol suggested that she live with them in Brompton, near Northallerton. They had a four-bedroom property set in five acres of land, with room to store Mary's furniture in their sheds. She was thrilled. Keith arranged a furniture van for the following week, and the family set away helping her pack. She had anticipated that it would be emotional leaving the bungalow, particularly when stripping the sitting room of its history and good memories. However, with so many hands on deck, there was no time for sentiment. It seemed that, suddenly, Mary was standing in an empty home. At 56 years old, she was saying goodbye to the home she had built and the life she knew. All her belongings were gone, save a few essentials which she could fit in the car. A week later, she closed the door of 2 Fuchsia Grove for the last time and took a leap of faith into the unknown.

It was wonderful to have the worry over where she was going to live taken away so quickly. However, after three months the travelling began to take its toll. Carol lived 25 miles out of Stockton, so Mary's journey back and forwards to do her voluntary work was clocking up at least 50 miles a day.

'I see less of you now than I did when you had your own place,' Carol laughed, but only half in jest. It was true, Mary barely saw her because she would be up and out before any of the family started getting up, and then it would be gone eleven o'clock most nights by the time she returned home.

She decided she would have to start doing something about it. Walking into the estate agents, she enquired about 10 Hartburn Lane again.

'Impossible,' the assistant said, barely lifting her eyes from the papers on the desk in front of her.

'But have you seen it? It's in a dreadful state of repair. It's worth nowhere near what you're asking for it.'

'We've told you, Mrs Butterwick, the vendor won't accept that price,' she replied, standing up from the desk and walking away. It was clear to Mary that she didn't want to talk to her. This avoidance was getting as bad as the response she faced from the hospital doctors. Still, every time she passed by the door she went in and asked, and every time she was told the same thing, until the following week, when she was dealt a harder blow.

'Oh, that place. Yes, there's an offer on it so you can forget it now,' the girl smirked, looking over at her colleague knowingly.

'Well, maybe they've not seen it,' Mary replied. 'It's not worth that money. You'll have to reduce it and come down to a fair honest price. Here is my friend's telephone number, should you need to get in touch.'

Mary didn't want to believe that there was another buyer; she *couldn't* believe it. In her mind, she had so many plans for that house. The ground floor would be the day care centre, she would live on the second floor and she would convert the attic into bedrooms so that her grandchildren could come and stay. She had looked at a few other houses, but nothing filled her with the same excitement as that one. 'We'll see if it sells,' she told herself.

Meanwhile, the travel was becoming too much and, out of physical weariness, she would find herself taking up offers from friends and people she visited to stay with them for the night. She often woke up on a sofa, wondering where she was. If she'd stopped to think about what she was doing, she never would've done it; but she didn't stop. Mary just lived from one day to the next, one meal to the next, and if that was a cup of tea and a piece of cake, that was good enough for her. The way she saw it, even if she didn't have a home to call her own, she always had a roof over her head and never went hungry. In that sense, she had all that she needed.

'I'm all right,' she told Carol. 'Just leave me to get on with it. I'll come back here when I need to.'

To Mary, where she was going to live was a small problem in comparison to those she saw every day in her voluntary work. There was much ignorance about cancer. It was known as 'the dirty big C', and, as far as she could see, the doctors and nurses weren't doing much to change that view.

'Do you know, I saw a lassie scrubbing a mug I'd given her a cup of tea in today,' she told Jo, who was familiar with such stories from her own counselling experience. 'I said: "What on earth are you doing?" "I don't want to give you cancer, Mary," she said. Can you believe that? That poor girl thought that she could spread her cancer. She thought it was contagious, and has been worried about giving it to someone else. Can you believe no one had even told her that much?'

The phone rang. 'Mary, it's for you,' said Jo.

'That's a bit odd I'm here, isn't it?' she laughed, taking the phone. 'Hello, Mary speaking.'

To her surprise it was the estate agent. 'Are you still interested in 10 Hartburn Lane, Mrs Butterwick?'

'Yes, but at the price I offered. I'm just waiting for a call from you, really.'

'Oh, right,' the agent sounded surprised. 'Well, the vendor says if it's still going to be a cash sale, the house is yours for the price you asked.'

'Great – it's a deal then! I'll call in as soon as I can.' She put down the phone and looked at Jo. 'That was the estate agent. I can have Hartburn Lane. Halleluiah!'

Now it was real, Mary was bursting to share her good news with all of her friends. Volunteering with the disabled group was still very much a part of her life, and, before the next meeting, she collected Val in her car and drove them round to see her new house.

'What do you think?' she asked excitedly, as her eyes scanned the front room, dreaming of what 10 Hartburn Lane could be.

'Are you thinking of buying *this* house, Mary?' Val asked, hesitantly.

'*Thinking* of buying it? I've bought it!' she said, quickly. 'Come – let me show you.'

Val stood still. 'What?' Mary asked, impatiently.

'Give over,' Val laughed. 'You're pulling my leg!'

'I'm not. I've had my eye on this place for ages. I put an offer in about 18 months ago and finally it's been accepted.'

'You mean you sold your lovely dorma bungalow to move in here? Are you mad?'

'I know it needs a little bit of work doing.'

'A little bit of work? My foot almost went through the floorboards when we came in, they're that rotten! And there's a great big tree growing through the sitting room!'

Mary looked around, her friend had a point. She had forgotten just what a state the place was in. Aside from the tree roots that had begun to grow through the wall, there was damp in the hall, iron bars on the kitchen window, no central heating and every room was in urgent need of decoration. 'Okay – try to forget what it looks like for now.' Val opened her mouth as if to interrupt, but Mary stopped her. 'Just wait a minute. Think about how it feels. There is such an incredible feeling of peace here, don't you think?'

Val smiled, resignedly. Reaching in her pocket, Mary pulled out a piece of paper. 'Here, read this and tell me what you think.'

'What is it?'

'Well, read it and find out.'

Val started reading. It was the idea Mary had penned – two years ago now – about the house. Val looked around at the crumbling walls and empty fire grate, then tried to imagine the place transformed through Mary's eyes. If she pulled this off it would be amazing, but how on earth was she going to manage it? Handing back the paper, she looked her friend in the eye and smiled: 'Well, Mary, if anyone can do it, you can.'

20

A DREAM, COME TRUE

Mary looked around at the chaos of her new home. 'If only living were as easy as dreaming,' she sighed. Mary had bought the house on its potential but she didn't have the first idea of how to start to fulfil that potential. John had always been the one who sorted out anything to do with their house, including the bills. Mary had never even written a cheque out while he was alive. Was it any wonder her friends thought she was going crazy? There was no escaping it – this was going to cost.

First, the house had to be rewired completely. Then there was dry rot and woodworm which needed to be treated, before she even started on new windows, guttering, chimney stacks and removing that tree. Luckily, after advice from friends, Mary managed to secure a grant for a damp course, and, slowly, the house started to become habitable. Yet, as autumn approached, the need for central heating became ever more pressing.

She called her cousin, Peggy, in Southport, whose husband, Trevor, ran a one-man plumbing business. The pair had grown up together, and Mary trusted her like a sister.

'Why have you bought a dump like this? It's madness!' said Trevor, when he saw the place.

'Everybody says the same, but I've bought it now,' said Mary. 'I know it needs central heating, but I'm so confused with these estimates – they go from one extreme to another. Can you tell which one is reasonable and good? Are some people robbing me, or are some people doing a shoddy job?'

'It's a heck of a job this, because it's a three-storey house,' he said, shaking his head. 'You've got 12 rooms or more. It's not going to be a tuppence ha'penny job.'

Despite all his bluster, Trevor offered to do the job himself. Once he'd finished the job he was working on, he would take a month off, come to Teesside with Peggy and 'sort this mess out', as he'd say.

Until then, Mary had to make do with a calor gas heater to heat the one habitable room in the house. There wasn't much furniture, and the floorboards were still bare. She stuffed newspapers around the window in an attempt to keep in the heat; she had read this as a tip in a magazine, but it didn't seem to be helping a great deal. 'I must be getting soft in my old age,' she laughed to herself, as she climbed into her sleeping bag still dressed in jeans and a sweater. She slept on a camp bed, next to which she had a small reading lamp and woollen bobble hat, which she pulled firmly over her ears before settling down to sleep. How on earth she'd managed in the days before central heating, she couldn't remember.

When she woke in the morning, her mind was racing. Peggy and Trevor couldn't stay in this house, no way. That day, she ran around making arrangements for them to stay with Carol. She could drive Trevor to and from the house every day, and there was a lovely café on Church Road where they could all have a hearty meal at the end of the day.

'Woah! Slow down,' Trevor laughed, when Mary began telling him her plans. 'If I'm going to do this job for you I want to get up and started on it first thing every morning. There is no way I want to be travelling to start the job. So, whatever we have to do, we're sleeping in that house.'

'But there are no carpets on the floor,' Mary explained.

'It's okay, I've seen it. I'm not expecting the Ritz! We'll manage.'

It could have been the most uncomfortable of times, but Mary had to admit that she was enjoying herself more than she had in a very long time. Much of that feeling came from being so close to Peggy again, and there was plenty of time to catch up while Trevor worked hard to bring the warm cosiness into the house that Mary had first envisaged.

The three of them slept on put-up beds in the same room. Every morning, Mary would boil the kettle on a small gas stove in the corner of the room to make tea. While Trevor worked, the women would go out and buy some basic essentials to make sandwiches for lunch. By five o'clock, it was time to wind down. Trevor would clean himself up and the three would saunter over to the nearby café, where Mary's friend prepared a warming three-course meal for them. After eating, they would often go for a walk in the local park, sharing memories and dreams, before returning to the house and its one habitable room, where they would try to rest before starting all over again the next day.

As Trevor had estimated, the plumbing and heating work was finished one month later. Mary paid Trevor for the materials but he refused to take any money for the labour, no matter how much she pressed him. Mary later sent him a cheque for the work, but it was never cashed.

Mary couldn't thank her cousins enough. Now she was on her way. The house as she had envisioned it was beginning to take shape. The joy of this realisation seemed to give her a burst of energy and, single-handedly, she began stripping the wallpaper from every room in the house. She felt like she didn't really know what she was doing, but somehow it all seemed to be coming together very well.

There was still much work to be done on the house, but Mary never seemed to get distracted by this fact. She'd managed to get a government grant to help pay for a damp proof course, but the builder she hired to do it uncovered dry rot and woodworm that needed to be treated, and also recommended a full electrical re-wire and re-plastering. Outside, there were repairs to do on the roof, all the windows needed to be replaced, the chimney stack had to be re-pointed and the house needed new drainpipes and guttering. Mary paid for the work as she went along, yet she wasn't prepared for the final bill.

'How much?' She couldn't believe it. Mary knew that it had taken a lot of work to put the house right, but how it had racked up to £6,000, she couldn't say. The builder went through the various amounts with her on the invoice, and it turned out his calculations were correct. In all, she had spent almost £30,000 getting 10 Hartburn Lane into a liveable condition, and that was before any decorating.

Mary knew that she didn't have enough money left to pay this bill, let alone buy the carpets and everything else that was needed to make the house a home. There were other implications too, for she knew the centre would never be able to get charitable status with a debt hanging over it. 'Perhaps it hadn't been such a good idea after all,' she chided herself.

That night, Mary prayed for confirmation that she was doing the right thing. 'Please, Lord, if this is the right thing to do, show me a way.'

It was some days later that Mary got her answer. In her role as a counsellor to cancer patients she was visiting a woman, Jean, who was desperate to talk to Mary, but away from her own home. Hartburn Lane was the only place she could think of where they would have any real privacy. Mary had grown used to the bare floors and walls, but bringing someone else into her home made her realise just how sparsely she had been living. She gave Jean the only chair in the house and pulled up a stool next to her. Jean was so distressed that she barely noticed her surroundings. Mary realised that the tears weren't only for her illness – there was so much going on in her life that she needed to unburden. It always amazed Mary how cruel people could be, especially when someone was so low already. Sometimes it was a reaction to that person's own pain and inability to cope with a loved one's illness, she reasoned, but that didn't make it any easier for those suffering at such behaviour.

Jean was desolate. She had revealed her darkest secrets, and there was no going back on that vulnerability. 'This poor woman has nothing left,' thought Mary. 'I need to offer something in return.'

Mary made them both a cup of tea while Jean washed her face and gathered her strength to re-face the world outside.

'Jean, you've shared so much with me. Is it okay if I share something with you?' Mary asked gently.

Jean looked at her, surprised. 'Yes, of course.'

'You think I'm going to live in this house, don't you?'

'Well, that's what you're getting it ready for, Mary,' she answered, confused.

'Yes, but you don't really know the truth of the matter.'

Mary then began to tell Jean about her idea for a day care centre
and how she hoped it would help both patients and their families.
'But the problem is, I've got this debt and I don't know what to do for
the best. I've not got the money, but I'll have to get it from
somewhere if I'm going to carry on. But do I carry on, or do I just
cut my losses now? I don't know.'

'You do,' said Jean sincerely. 'You know what you've got to do.'

'I don't. You tell me?' said Mary shaking her head.

'You've got to carry on, Mary,' she said. 'Because if this house helps
anyone else like it's helped me today, then you know you've got to
carry on.'

Mary took Jean's hands in hers and smiled. 'Well, that's sorted.
We'll carry on, won't we?'

When she spoke those words, there was no doubt in Mary's mind
that she was going to try to make it work. She'd had her answer, and,
as she'd come to realise, God's answers weren't always the most
straightforward. She still didn't know how she would make it work,
but she had faith that somehow she would.

Of course there was still money to be spent, but where money
could be saved it had to be. To this end, Mary enlisted friends and a
group of youth training scheme boys to help paint the house both
inside and out, while Reg agreed to use his joinery skills to help out
with a few handyman jobs, like fixing door handles. The paint came
from a competition Jo had spotted in a local advertisement – by sheer
coincidence a large firm was giving away the chance to win several
tins of paint, the catch being that you had to write and explain how it
would be used. Mary penned her entry and, within a couple of
weeks, she was whooping down the phone in delight on being told
she was the winner. She didn't know where Reg got the wood from,
but he carved out a little chapel in the wide hallway that was more
beautiful than she could ever have imagined.

Mary was sure that everyone thought her slightly mad, but the fact
that they were still there supporting her touched her heart and gave
her the motivation to carry on, even if her friends did tease her on
occasions. Like the time the vicar, Stephen Pedley, called round and

he'd no sooner stepped through the door than she'd shouted down the stairs: 'Come up to my bedroom, vicar.'

'Poor Stephen's face – he didn't know where to look!' Val laughed.

'Well, look at the state of this place – it's the only room where you can sit down,' Mary reasoned, her seriousness making Val laugh all the harder.

Not that Mary noticed. The house was moving forward so fast now that there was much that passed her by. Like when Arthur said he loved her. Where had that come from? She hadn't seen it coming, but, looking back, perhaps she should have done. She would do nothing to hurt her good friend, Arthur, not intentionally, but she couldn't love him back in the way that he wanted. He hadn't been round to visit her since that night; she did miss him. He'd left a gap in her life, but it wasn't enough to change her heart towards him. Not like Tom. Now, Tom was a man she could love in that way, if only she would let herself. She closed her eyes and remembered the rush she'd felt as he grabbed her hand when they ran across the road to catch the bus. It was like an electric bolt through her very being, shocking her back to life. She had always held hands with John whenever they were out. Now, for the first time since his death, she had felt alive; she had felt like a woman again and it was liberating.

Falling in love a second time, however, was a lot more compli-cated, or at least it felt that way. Mary wasn't a teenager any more, and there were so many other things that needed her time and attention. The house had to come first. It was so close now that the focus had to be on getting it open. Of course, this wasn't an easy choice. Some things, she realised, never changed with age.

There was more heartache when the Coping with Cancer group, with which she had been so closely involved, informed her that they didn't want anything to do with the house. Mary was devastated. These weren't just acquaintances turning their back on her now, they were her friends. It was the debt that was making them nervous, she reasoned, but it didn't make the pain of rejection any less.

Still, she couldn't let this blow destroy her dream. Okay, so she couldn't get charity status; for now, she would concentrate on what she *could* do. It didn't matter how many people told her that it wouldn't work, or asked snidely: 'Who do you think you are?' She would continue. While volunteering in the hospital, doctors would say: 'This house of yours, do you think it'll succeed?' Or sometimes the comments were more defensive: 'Do you think you'll get away with this, Mary?'

Mary knew she would have to prove herself before she could gain any trust, especially from within the medical community. Yet, no matter what obstacles they raised, she was determined to overcome them. Mary was convinced that the house would help. She saw the need for it acutely every day, walking alongside cancer patients, taking them for treatment, talking to them and holding them while they cried. In her mind, she couldn't separate the family from the patient. By helping one, she was helping the other. Why did so many people fail to see what to her was so obvious? Why were some medical staff so dismissive of the idea of the home? These were caring people in a caring profession, and she believed that deep down some of them must have thought about these same issues too. She started speaking in church halls and at Women's Institutes, telling anyone who would listen what it was she was trying to do.

Finally, just before Christmas, the house was ready. To celebrate, Mary invited Stephen to bless the house. This was the same man who, on so many occasions, had told her to go home and forget the idea. She didn't blame him, really. He wasn't the only one who had thought it sounded a bit crazy – indeed, that *she* sounded a bit crazy. Time after time, she would knock on his door and tell him about the idea she had for this house and how it could help people. Now it was really happening, Stephen was one of the first to accept that on this he might have been wrong. It still sounded like an utopian idea, but if the church couldn't support an idealistic world, then who would? Besides, he was only agreeing to bless the house and it would have been churlish to refuse such a request.

There were no formal invitations, but Mary told everyone she bumped into: 'I'm having the house blessed. You're very welcome to come along. There will be food and drinks afterwards.'

Mary had no idea how many people to expect, which was probably just as well, because once the doorbell started ringing it never stopped. There must have been 300 people in the house that night. People of all faiths and some of none, united in their wish for the house to succeed, to bring care and humanity to a world that sometimes seemed to have lost direction.

She wanted to welcome everyone personally, but it was over-whelming. 'Here,' a man said, pushing an envelope into her hand.

'What's that?' she asked.

'I don't know. It's from Albert Dicken. He said he couldn't stop but to make sure that I gave it to you.'

Mary put it in her pocket. She was sorry to have missed Albert. He was a successful businessman who ran a chain of DIY stores. She knew him through her church, and he'd always been supportive of her idea. She scanned the many faces gathered inside her house. Arthur wasn't there. She hoped he was okay. He must be so lonely, she thought. There was no Tom either, although, considering the delicate state of her heart, she thought this was probably for the best.

'Mary!' It was Mrs Fordham, the leader of the voluntary group. She embraced her in a big hug, and suddenly didn't seem such a fearsome sergeant major anymore. 'Well done!' she beamed.

'Thank you, Mrs Fordham,' Mary said, genuinely touched.

'I've only got one thing to say to you now.' Mary didn't know where this was going, but she let her continue. 'Don't you ever dare call me Mrs Fordham again! I'm Elsie to you from this day on.'

'Okay, Elsie it is,' Mary said, smiling, although the words seemed strange.

'And another thing,' she added. 'Don't you ever dream of going anywhere else for your materials to help these people. I'll supply them!' Mary caught Reg's eye and he smiled knowingly.

It wasn't until she closed the door on the last guest that it finally hit her: 'I've done it. There is no going back now, this is it!'

She felt in her pocket, and pulled out the envelope from Albert. Inside was a cheque for £250, and a note with a verse from St Paul's letter to the Philippians:

My God will fulfil all your needs out of the riches of his glory in Christ Jesus.

Mary smiled in agreement. Of that, she was now sure.

Part 4

WATCHING LOVE GROW

21

UNFORESEEN BATTLES

The day care centre was up and running, but Mary knew that there was still much to be done if it was to become the dream she had hoped for. She had managed to get funding for one full-time nurse and three part-time staff, who took care of the cooking, cleaning and anything else that needed doing. It was all hands on deck and everyone helped everyone else. Outside of staff wages, Mary funded the centre from her pension of £39 a week – £10 of which she spent on petrol, visiting and fetching patients.

The way her money was stretched, it sometimes felt like she was going back to the make do and mend years of the war. Four ham shanks from the butchers lasted a week, being made into soup, sandwiches and omelettes for patients. Nothing was wasted, but that didn't mean there were no treats. There was always home-made cake at tea time and freshly baked scones in the morning.

'I'm sure you've got a magic purse,' Val joked one day.

'Waste not, want not,' Mary laughed. 'It's second nature to me after the war. Back then we wouldn't even throw out a bit of string or brown paper – we would iron them out and use them again.'

Val, being much younger, had never experienced the rationing of war time, but while she laughed she also marvelled at the way Mary seemed to make everything last without being miserly. When she said 'want not', she meant it. Not one patient or member of staff ever went hungry in that house, and it was always good wholesome food. Mary would say: 'If they can't get any solid food down, hopefully they can manage a little soup and get some goodness that way. It's all fresh vegetables and good protein from the meat.'

After closing the day care centre for the night, Mary would sit at her portable type-writer, writing letters and leaflets about what the house was intended for and the work they were doing there. To save money on stamps, she would later walk round town, posting information through letter boxes, trying to get the message out in the cheapest way possible.

She advocated diversional therapy, which meant giving patients something to take their mind off their illness. It was about creating a more positive attitude to life, letting the dying know that they were still living and that this space between living and dying was there to be filled with good things. Life could still be enjoyed. Like the doctors, she accepted that patients would die, as we all have to, but this house was about living – really living – until we die.

Of course, her ideas weren't always embraced. 'What is it exactly that you are trying to do with this house of yours, Mary?' one doctor asked, dismissively.

'I'm just trying to show that there is much more to a person than an illness, and that patients should be looked after as a whole – mind, body and spirit.'

'What are you trying to say?'

Mary felt that this consultant, like most of the others, didn't really want to listen.

'I'm not trying to say anything,' Mary said, adding in her head: 'Apart from the fact that you've lost all sense of reasoning.'

'That's strange, because I'd heard you had plenty to say on how we treat patients here. Maybe now you're doing it you finally realise it's not as easy at it looks.'

Mary bit her tongue. This was a doctor who had trained for years to know what was best for patients, she reasoned. In his eyes, how dare a woman with no training claim she might know better?

She went into the chapel to pray. It was a month since the day care centre had opened, and already she had seen so much goodness from it. Surely it couldn't simply be that she wanted so much for it to work that she was *imagining* it was?

She felt someone sit down beside her; too close for someone who wanted a private prayer in an empty chapel. Mary looked up.

'Sorry to disturb you.'

Mary didn't know who the woman was, but from her uniform she recognised her as a district nurse.

'I just wanted to say that you are the first person with any courage in this community.'

'What do you mean?'

'This house that you've opened – it's going to be the best thing since sliced bread.'

'Do you reckon?' Mary asked, smiling, grateful for the reassurance.

'I know it will be, but it's taken someone like you to have the courage to do it.'

It soon became apparent that it *was* working, for it wasn't just patients asking to come in, but district nurses too would often show up, asking to borrow mattresses or other equipment that they couldn't get hold of easily elsewhere. The running of the day care began to expand into other areas of the house. The ground floor had always been intended for the day care, the second floor as living quarters and the third floor as storage space for equipment and eventually a place for Mary's family to come and stay. However, Mary's sitting and dining rooms on the second floor were soon taken over by offices, and she found herself, once again, living in the one bedroom in which she'd started, converting the adjacent dressing room into a small kitchen for her own use.

The debt was paid off gradually in chunks of £200 – each £10 donated raising cheers in the office. Six months after opening, Carol's solicitor, John Richardson, who had advised Mary legally during the set up, delighted in announcing that the centre was now debt-free and could apply for charitable status.

'Your next decision is who will be the Trustees,' he told Mary.

'Well we don't want a lot,' she answered quickly. 'Too many people just means that it takes longer to get any decisions made.'

John laughed warmly. 'I'd say half a dozen would be sufficient.'

After much explaining, Mary convinced Stephen Pedley to sit on the Board of Trustees. He had listened to Mary's idea for more than a year, hoping that eventually she would forget all about it. He had thought her the most unlikely person to be able to pull something like this off, but once he saw her commitment in practice he was happy to offer his support.

Stephen was joined on the Board by Mary's son-in-law, Tony Huck, her nurse friend, Jean Alderman, and a sympathetic doctor, Richard Douglass, who, once the day care was up and running, had surprised Mary with his openness to her vision. Albert Dicken was to be the chairman, leaving space on the Board for just one more.

Mary took the list to her solicitor. 'What about you? You're not on this list,' he observed.

'Yes – there's me,' Mary said quickly. 'But I'm not in the six. Which only leaves one to go,' she paused briefly. 'I was thinking, what about you as a solicitor?'

'Oh! At last – I thought you were never going to ask,' he smiled.

Tom was coming over for supper and Mary couldn't wait to tell him the good news: – the John Butterwick Day Care Centre was now officially the John Butterwick Trust.

Despite Mary's initial reluctance, she had started to accept that she too had feelings. Tom had made her feel whole again after John's death, like she really mattered. She wanted to share her joy with him; she wanted to share everything with him.

It was eight o' clock in the evening and the dinner was in the oven, but it would be all but ruined now. Where was he? By eight-thirty, she started to get worried and was all ready for driving round to his house to check he was okay when the phone rang.

'Mary, it's me.'

'Tom! What's happened? Are you okay?'

'Yes, I'm fine. I was just calling to say that I won't be able to make it round tonight.'

'Why? Are you okay?'

'I'm fine. I'm at Billingham Green so I can't talk now. I'll call you tomorrow.'

Before she could ask for any more explanation, he was gone. She rescued what was left of the dinner and, although her appetite wasn't what it was earlier, she ate it rather than waste it.

The next day there was no time for self-pity. Tom was busy; it was as simple as that. Waiting for the phone to ring was what she might expect her grand-daughter to be doing, not a 60-year-old woman like herself. Besides, there was much to be done.

Now the centre had charity status, she could start fundraising to support the work properly. She began with coffee evenings. Such events were cheap to put on – all you needed was to boil a kettle and buy some nice biscuits – but, from this, they could raise £200 in one evening. Mary loved how these evenings provided a sense of community, giving something back rather than simply asking for money. That was important to Mary, for she knew that if someone didn't receive anything in return for their giving, it would soon stop. This she found was also true for volunteers. She would always sit and talk to anyone who offered to help out, explaining what was involved. 'You've got to feel right about this and there has got to be something for you in this too,' she'd say. 'If you don't receive anything then very soon you won't give anything. You've got to get something out of it yourself, or else you'll be miserable. It's like anything – if it's right for you and you put your butt into it, it'll turn out good. I've always got so much more out of volunteering than I could ever give in return.' From the large number of volunteers helping out, Mary could only guess that the house *was* giving them something in return, for which she was truly amazed and grateful.

It was only a month until Christmas, and Mary knew that meant money would be tight for a lot of people. Being practically-minded, she reasoned that people would still be sending Christmas cards, but she would have to be quick if she was to produce and sell her own. A friend had painted a wonderful picture of Stockton Town Hall, to which she'd given Mary the rights. The only trouble was that she felt that it wasn't very Christmassy. It needed something else.

At the same time, Alf, a patient, had begun to use the paints that were provided as part of the crafts in the day care centre to paint pictures of delicate little flowers, which everyone admired.

'Alf, those flowers you paint – do you think you could do some more and we can sell them?'

'What these daft little things?' he laughed. 'I don't think anyone would pay for these.'

'Alf, they're beautiful – everyone says so.'

He looked slightly embarrassed at the compliment. 'Well, if you think so – it's nothing to me to paint a few more.'

'Wonderful,' Mary beamed. 'We can make little gift tags out of them, and sell them to raise money for the centre.'

'Really?'

'Yes, of course! And another thing, I've been given this picture to use as a Christmas card but it's not very Christmassy. Do you think you could work on something for the inside – some holly and mistletoe, and write *Happy Christmas*?'

'If you're sure that's what you want.'

'Marvellous.'

Mary was delighted, and was thrilled to find the rest of the staff shared her excitement. It had been a wonderful day.

Mary said goodbye to the staff, finished clearing up and went upstairs to start on the admin which, although important, she had found no time for during the day. 'Don't you ever go to bed, Mary? Only, I see your light on very late,' people would always remark.

'I'm all right. Don't you worry about me,' she'd reply, genuinely. There was a lot to do, but seeing the centre grow and succeed gave her the energy to continue.

Mary sat at her typewriter. She'd been asked to write an article about the centre for her parish magazine. Normally she had so much to say about it, but this time the words wouldn't come.

As she sat wondering what to say, the doorbell rang. Answering it her spirits lifted and dropped at the same time. 'So, the wanderer returns!'

'Can I come in?' Tom asked, ignoring her sarcasm.

'Of course,' she moved aside and he followed her in.

They made small talk while Mary boiled the kettle for tea, but both of them knew something had changed.

After about ten minutes, Tom finally said what they were both thinking. 'This isn't working, is it, Mary?'

'What do you mean?' she said, buying time.

'Oh, come on,' he sighed. 'Us – how can it?'

'Well it can't if you're going to not show up and then disappear for a couple of days.'

'That's rich coming from you,' he muttered.

'What's that?'

Tom wasn't up for a fight. 'Okay, I was out of order, I accept that – I'm sorry,' he conceded. 'But, looking forward, where can we go? You're married to the centre and that's fine, but I'm looking for a wife who'll be married to me first, and I think we both know that's never going to happen.'

Mary was angry and upset. Deep down she knew he was right, but it still hurt. Tom felt pushed out in a way, and, when she looked at it objectively, who could blame him? In time, she would look back on their 12 months together with a fondness, knowing that each had fulfilled a special need in the other, while understanding too why their relationship had to end. She couldn't see that tonight, of course. Tonight was for tears. Tom had awakened in her the multitude of tiny ways in which we can love and miss somebody.

It was for those that she cried. Oh, how she missed John.

22

SMALL MIRACLES

Mary read the handwritten note from her nurse, Stella Kruger, and smiled. For days, she had been puzzling over how to explain the house in an article for her parish magazine, and now here was her answer.

I get tremendous job satisfaction, and have achieved a fulfilment I never thought possible, Stella had written. *It is upsetting when one of our visitors dies, but generally there is no sadness in this house – just a lot of camaraderie.*

It was how Mary had imagined it originally, but now she realised that she couldn't have written this because it wasn't simply about her dream any more. The place had become bigger than that; it was about the staff and the patients now – what it could do and was doing for their lives, and, while she might have ideas of what she would like in this respect, she couldn't second guess or guarantee it. Realising this, Mary had asked her staff and a couple of the patients if they would mind writing something down about what the house meant to them.

Marion Brookes, one of the part-time staff members, wrote:

I feel guilty getting paid. Before working here, I had done voluntary work for about ten years, and I have always been interested in helping others. Mary is a wonderful person who helps everyone in so many ways. I've made so many new friends here and Mary is such a good listener that you can talk to her about anything.

Under her note was another, written by Alf, with one of his signature small flowers drawn carefully on the bottom right hand corner of the paper.

Alf was a Londoner. His wife had died several years earlier, and, when he was diagnosed with terminal cancer, he moved to the North-east to be nearer to his son. It was unfortunate circumstances that, around the same time, his daughter-in-law was unwell and the day care centre had provided welcome respite for all the family.

Like his paintings, Alf's note was simple, but beautiful:

Thank you to everyone at the John Butterwick Day Care Centre. For the first time in a very long time I feel fulfilled as a human being.

One year on, and the day care centre was no longer a dream, it was a wonderful reality. There was so much to be thankful for. Mary closed her eyes, her heart filled with love and she smiled 'Thank you, Lord.'

23

A NEW DREAM

The John Butterwick Day Care Centre was now in its second year, and Mary no longer had to fight as hard to be heard. Of course there were still the sceptics, but their voices no longer drowned out the many who were singing its praises. Even in the hospital, some of the doctors were beginning to comment positively. 'This seems to be going well, Mary?', they would say, clearly wanting to know more.

Mary had tapped into a need to receive care, but she couldn't have imagined the capacity for giving the house would open in the surrounding community. There was no shortage of volunteers ready to put the fun into fundraising, and no end of support from the people of Teesside.

The first May Day Fair at Norton Green had been a huge success. They'd dressed up in silly wigs and costumes, baked cakes and set up bric-a-brac stalls, tombolas, games – anything they could think of.

Even the mayor was impressed. 'There must be thousands of people here today, Mary,' he said, clearly amazed, adding: 'You really must do this again.' Not being one to miss an opportunity, Mary set a date for the following year – this family fair would become an annual event.

The day care centre continued to grow in strength and, although it kept Mary busy, it began to run itself. For this, Mary was thankful, because her energy reserves were getting low. It had been a year of personal sadness. Her nephew, Alec, the son of her dear cousins, Peggy and Trevor, had hanged himself. Distraught, his parents left England soon after, to be nearer their daughter in Australia. How Mary would miss them both.

Around the same time, Mary's mother, Hilda, died of kidney failure after a short stay in hospital, where Mary found the care had not improved significantly since John's death. Aged 87, Hilda walked with the aid of a stick. Mary had taken this into the hospital for her, but when Hilda asked for it she'd been refused. She had also fallen out of bed, something Mary found hard to forgive of those meant to be caring for her. It came back to dignity and quality of life – the fight for which had motivated her to open the day care in the first place. Why was such simple humanity so hard to express?

This double loss, coupled with yet another example of institutional neglect, was almost too much to bear. Once again, there were so many questions with so few answers. Was she wasting her time trying to change things? She got into her car and drove to the only place where she thought she might begin to piece herself back together; hopefully Kath would be in when she got there.

After a few days in Scotland under the care of her great friend, Mary was beginning to feel ready to return to the day care. Walking along Sinclair's Bay, it felt like the fresh winds from the North Sea were catching her worries and blowing them away. They cleared her mind like nothing else. She never tired of staring out across the seemingly endless water; it was entrancing, and sometimes Mary wanted to be entranced. Worry was useless, she knew that, but, being human, it was so easy to get caught up in 'what if's? She reminded herself that there was a reason that God asks us to live one day at a time. Each day has its own troubles. If she trusted in him, she would have the strength to cope with problems as they arose. No one can cope with their life's troubles, or even a month's troubles, in a day. Trying to do so would be overwhelming. Indeed, she had been feeling overwhelmed, so much so that she was beginning to lose the joy in her life.

She took off her shoes and socks to feel the sand under her feet. Recently she had felt so much pain that she had become numb. It was almost as if her body couldn't cope with any more emotion and so had decided not to feel at all. Rolling her trousers up above her knees, Mary ran into the sea. The drop in temperature caused her to catch her breath. It was icy, but it was real. There was still much to be thankful for: her four beautiful children (how she loved them all), her kind and generous friends, who had and continued to support her,

Kath's never-failing comfort, the love and laughter in the day care, the encouraging words from staff and patients, the beauty all around her which she had allowed herself to become blind to, the healing power of nature and the goodness of God. It was on these things, on these many things, that she now had to focus.

On the walk back to Kath's house, Mary started to recall the wonderful weekends spent as a family at Roseberry Topping in North Yorkshire. Her dear brother Jack used to rent a small chalet there. Well, 'chalet' was a bit of a grand description – it was a wooden hut up in the hills – but she couldn't have loved it more had it been a castle. Being there gave her the same sense of freedom she felt here in the North East of Scotland. There are magnificent 360-degree views from the summit of Roseberry Topping; on a clear day you can see as far as the Yorkshire Dales in one direction and Teesside in the other. Seeing so much space used to free Mary to think about the obstacles she found in her life in a different way. It was as if, looking to the horizon, she could see beyond the problems of today and knew that everything would be okay.

When Jack decided to give up the rent on the chalet, Mary asked if he would please see if she could have it. It only had two bedrooms and a small kitchen with a big pot sink in the corner, but it was a huge step up from the tent her family was used to, and, while it was often a struggle to pay the rent, it was worth it. Mary smiled, remembering John sitting on the balcony and the children sat around him, engrossed in his adventure stories.

Mary's mother had left her a small amount of money in her will. Perhaps she could use it to find somewhere similar here, a little retreat in Scotland where she could come and recharge her batteries? Of course, she knew that she could always stay with Kath, but if she was going to be visiting more often she certainly didn't want to keep putting her friend out of her own bed. Kath, now a widow too, lived in a one-bedroom bungalow. When Mary came to stay, she insisted on giving her the bed and she would sleep on the floor. No matter how much Mary argued against it, Kath stayed firm: 'You're my guest, Mary, and I won't hear of you sleeping on the floor. You've come all this way to see me, so you sleep in the bed and that's final.'

After some gentle persuasion, Kath agreed to keep her eyes open for any rental properties that might be suitable, and Mary returned home to Teesside feeling refreshed and ready to face the next challenges the day care centre would bring. Despite its critics, and Mary knew there always would be some, the centre was clearly fulfilling a need in the community. It was running far more smoothly now, but that didn't mean any less work. Often, she was asked: 'You do umpteen jobs and it doesn't seem to trouble you at all. How do you do it?'

As well as taking charge of the day care centre, she was filling in all the necessary paperwork, writing the newsletter and keeping up her voluntary work. Mary couldn't lie: it wasn't easy. It had taken her a long time to realise that no one can do it all, no matter how it looks to anyone on the outside. It was a case of doing one thing at a time – wearing one cap, then taking it off and putting on another for a completely different role. It was something Mary had learned from the Sisters of the Order of the Holy Paraclete, at Whitby.

Whenever she spent time at St Hilda's Priory, where the order was based, she was always amazed at how the Sisters could lay down whatever they were doing for prayer time and come back to it later. One minute she would be washing up with them in the kitchen, then the bell would go for prayer and they would have to lay the pots down, no matter how many were left, and go to prayer. They would come back to the dishes later. Mary found such simplicity wonderful and tried to apply it elsewhere in her life. So often, while at home, she had found herself getting aggravated, thinking: 'Oh, I haven't done this, or I must finish that.' In some ways, it was almost like she'd been telling herself that it was a life or death matter to get the washing up or ironing finished. Of course these things need to be done, but it was so easy to get their importance out of proportion.

Life with the Sisters had taught Mary how to prioritise tasks, how to concentrate on one thing at a time, to find time for God and, in doing so, to find time for others and for enjoying life. She began to learn how to reflect on her own words and actions, so that she could respond to others' needs better. The Sisters also helped her to be still, silent and open to hearing from God. Obviously this wasn't a voice as many people would recognise a voice; rather, it was a knowing, deep inside, almost like an instinct. She would take her problems to God in prayer and, in the stillness, he would give her the answers.

It was after much thought that she had decided to take up the offer of becoming a Tertiary Sister of the order. This meant that she would agree to put Christ at the centre of her life and to live by a certain set of rules, although her vocation would be out in the world rather than in the Whitby community. Soon she would be taking her final vows. It was what she wanted, but she did sometimes worry, asking her vicar, Stephen, if she was doing the right thing.

'I don't think I'm good enough,' she told him.

He laughed.

'I don't think it's anything to laugh about,' she added, seriously.

'Mary, what you've said just shows me that God has got you in his hands.'

'What do you mean?' she asked, genuinely puzzled.

'Well, neither am I good enough. We're all human. There is none of us perfect. It's when we start to believe we are that the trouble starts.'

It was what Mary needed to hear – the confirmation she had been seeking to go ahead and take her final vows. Often she felt that God used other people to guide her, to answer questions that she had brought in prayer. She felt that had begun to happen with the day care centre. Yes, it was doing well – indeed, many would say that it was an unmitigated success – but she had begun to feel that it needed something else.

'Can you tell me where I'm going to go to die?' asked George, a visitor to the centre, whose condition had deteriorated to the extent that Mary was now visiting him at his home in Eaglescliffe.

'I can't really answer that,' Mary said, honestly. 'I really wish I could, but I can't.'

George said nothing, but looked across the room as if looking into another land. Mary wanted desperately to help him. 'Okay, let's look at what your circumstances are. Have you got any family who could help you when that time comes?'

George was back with her. 'Yes, I have.'

'Well, go on then – who would you ask?'

'I don't know,' he said resignedly. 'I've got four kids but how can I ask any one of them? It wouldn't be fair to burden them with that. I couldn't do it.'

That night, Mary couldn't stop thinking about George and his situation. Mary tried to put herself in his position. She too had four children, but who would *she* ask? Who do you ask at a time like that? Besides, the other person has to really want to do it, to be there for you. Could his dilemma be her dilemma? If it were her, she would be terrified of dying alone.

Several times in recent months, Mary had been asked about beds for the terminally ill, somewhere for patients to go at the end of their life where they could die, pain-free and with dignity. This time it had struck a chord with her because, in George, she saw a part of herself, and she felt it deep in her heart. Although no one used the word, Mary began to realise that people were asking for a hospice. There were none in the North-east at that time, but it was an idea that Mary had recently come across in her reading.

She picked up the phone and started dialling the operator to get the nearest hospice. 'Leeds? Are you sure?' she asked, appalled at what she had found.

The operator was correct. The closest hospice to Teesside was Leeds. How could that benefit the patient, or their family? It was 50 miles away, almost two hours on the train, just to get into the centre, never mind having to get out to the hospice. It wasn't feasible to ask someone to travel that far. Her heart ached for George, but even if she couldn't help him, she was determined to make sure that in the future the Butterwick Trust would help others like him.

24

STARTING OVER

Mary was quite aware that deciding to open a hospice and actually opening one were two very different things. She was clear what she wanted it to be like. It would have the same ethos as the day care centre. It was, first and foremost, to be a place of love and care. It had to maintain its personal touch – ten beds seemed a reasonable number. However, to fund this many would cost far more money than they were currently spending on the day care centre. She would need to hire specialist palliative care nurses who would work round the clock.

When she started to tot up the cost, it felt like an impossible task, but she'd felt that before with the day care centre, and look where they were now. Whether she would succeed or fail in this, she couldn't say. All she did know was that, if it was to succeed, she would need the backing of the community. This wasn't to be her hospice, it would be *their* hospice, and if it was what the community wanted she would go all out to try to make it happen.

Mary persuaded the Trustees to hold an open meeting to discuss the possibility of expanding the day care centre into a hospice. She booked St Andrew and St George United Reformed Church on Yarm Lane in Stockton, and set about advertising it through posters, leaflets and word of mouth. By this time, word about the day care centre was beginning to spread outside of the Stockton area. So much so that Tyne Tees Television had brought a camera crew along to film a news item on the work they were doing. The owner of an electrical store on Yarm Road agreed to lend Mary two televisions for her to screen the film during the open meeting. The Trustees all took seats at the front, and the church began to fill until people were standing in the aisles. Mary could barely contain her joy, but it wasn't over yet — there was still much convincing to be done.

She stood up: 'We believe that Stockton and the surrounding district desperately needs a hospice. We care, and, judging by your attendance here tonight, I think that you do too. But if we are going to do it, we need your support, so we've come here tonight to explain exactly what we think we need, and to see if it's what you want too.'

Each of the Trustees followed her to speak, explaining, from their own area of expertise, why they were in support of opening a hospice in the area. It would of course mean moving out of the day care centre at Hartburn Lane to bigger premises. None of this would come cheap, but, if the community was behind it, then the Trustees were willing to start to look for another building and have a go at making it work.

After everyone had finished, Mary invited questions from the floor. Her stomach flipped as a district nurse stood up first. 'I don't know how it can be done, but I agree we do need this palliative care,' she said.

To Mary's amazement everyone clapped, and suddenly there was a chorus of agreement running through the hall. Then, after a couple of questions about the practicalities of such a project, Val stood on her chair in support and challenged everyone: 'Right, they've told us what *they* are going to do, now what are *you* going to do as a community? What are *you* – sitting on each chair – what are you as *individuals* going to do?'

Looking at her friend stood on the chair, fighting her corner already, made Mary smile. She couldn't hide her joy any longer, and it beamed out of her. It was clear that the community wanted beds. The people of Teesside wanted a hospice and they were going to support the Trust in providing one. Exactly how any of it would actually happen was a question for another day.

25

LIFE'S NOT ALWAYS WHAT IT SEEMS

'I've found it!' Kath squealed down the phone.

'Great, sounds exciting,' Mary replied, before adding quickly: 'What have you found?'

'Oh, Mary,' she sighed impatiently. 'Have you forgotten already?'

'What?' Mary was puzzled. She wasn't good at guessing games.

'The little getaway you wanted me to find for you, I've been looking and I think I've found one.'

'Well, glory be and alleluia! That's marvellous news!'

'Mary, it's just perfect. I know you'll love it.'

'Where is it?'

'It's right on the coast. You can see the sea from the window.'

Mary was so happy she thought she was going to cry. 'I'll take it!'

'You'll what?'

'I said I'll take it!"

'But you've not even seen it yet!'

'I trust you. It'll be fine. It's in my price range, yes?'

'Of course! It's everything you could want.'

'Wonderful! Can you tell them I'll take it, and I'll be up to collect the keys in a couple of weeks?'

Before then, Mary was due to take her vows to become a Tertiary Sister, which meant staying overnight with the Sisters at St Hilda's Priory in Whitby. There was also the task of finding a building to start the hospice. Plans to merge 10 Hartburn Lane with the house next door had fallen through. Not to be discouraged, Mary had already got an estate agent on the job. She could do no more for now, so had to lay that problem to one side and trust that it would work out for the best.

She was looking forward to going to Whitby. She had gained so much from being a part of the order, and now she was to make it official. She smiled to herself. It never ceased to amaze her how lives entwined in the most unexpected ways. She was thinking specifically about Sister Mary Aldred, from Burnham Abbey in Maidenhead, who she had met on a bus journey back from a visit to her daughter, Julia, in Hampton.

She had decided to take the bus between Middlesbrough and London – the longest part of the journey – rather than the car, purely for economic reasons after spotting an advert for a £14 return fare – going by car would have costed her at least £20 in petrol. Also, although she loved driving, since John's death she had found herself sometimes feeling overwhelmed with grief, which she knew wasn't safe on the motorway.

After a wonderful Easter weekend spent with Julia and her family, Mary said her goodbyes at Hampton and took a train back to London. However, in deciding to take the bus from there back home, she hadn't accounted on just how busy the station would be. It took some time just to find out which stop the Middlesbrough bus was leaving from. She looked at her watch – there was an hour before the bus was due to leave, and that was if it left on time. So many people, so much noise – no wonder people in London always seem stressed, she thought. There wasn't even anywhere to sit down, but, just as she was beginning to get flustered, Mary spotted a single seat left by the wall.

Mary nodded at the woman sitting in the next seat, said 'Good morning', and then tried to remove herself from the hustle and bustle by burying her head in a newspaper.

'Excuse me, dear, would you mind watching my bag while I go and find an inspector?'

Mary turned and looked at the woman, all dressed in black. How had she not noticed the woman was a nun when she sat down? 'We can miss the most obvious things when we're pre-occupied,' she thought.

The nun wandered around for a good ten minutes but couldn't find an inspector anywhere.

'Where are you going?' Mary asked on her return.

'I need to be in Middlesbrough to catch the four o'clock train from the station.'

'You'll be lucky if you get into Middlesbrough for six o'clock,' Mary said, honestly.

'Hmmm – that's going to make things difficult,' she said, although Mary noticed that Sister Mary Aldred didn't seem unduly troubled by the situation. Mary recognised that inner peace; that ability to not react in stress to everyday situations we can't control but desperately want to. It was a trait she so admired and aspired to, yet, just minutes before, she'd found herself getting wound up by what she could now see was simply a busy bus station.

'You wouldn't be going to Whitby on that four o'clock train, by any chance?' Mary asked.

'How did you know that? That's exactly where I'm going! I've just had quite a serious operation and I'm going there to convalesce.'

'Poor woman,' Mary thought. It turned out that she had already been on the road for hours. Her bus had been delayed and the driver had stopped five times to try to call the main depot to ask them to hold the connecting bus. Unfortunately, every public phone he tried was damaged or broken in some way and he wasn't able to get though. Sister Mary Aldred arrived at the bus station just to see her bus pulling away, and had no choice but to sit for hours until the next one. It looked like she wouldn't get to Whitby now until very late in the evening, if at all.

'I know I'm a total stranger, but when this bus comes to go to Middlesbrough, would you trust me to get you to Whitby?'

Sister Mary Aldred looked Mary in the eyes and paused slightly, before replying: 'Yes I would, but what do you suggest?'

'Okay. You're going to come to Stockton with me and, if you trust me, I'll see you get into Whitby before Compline. It's your only chance.'

Compline is the last service of the day, after which the nuns go to bed, and Mary knew it was important for the Sister to reach Whitby before that. Sister Mary Aldred smiled. 'How do you know about Compline?'

'If you must know, I'm planning to take my novice promises at St Hilda's, to become a Tertiary Sister.'

Sister Mary Aldred knew she was in good hands now. Her smile widened. 'Goodness gracious, isn't the Lord good!'

The pair had eventually got off the bus at Stockton, and ran across Stockton High Street to where Mary had left her car at the house of her mother, who was still alive at the time. Looking back, Mary marvelled at how her mother, ever patient, never seemed surprised, no matter who she turned up with. Mary burst into her mother's flat, a conversion of a Victorian house near the old YMCA, with Sister Mary Aldred in tow, and her mother never questioned either of them.

'Hi, Mother, are you okay? We're going to dash out again,' she said, turning to Sister Mary Aldred. 'There's the bathroom. I'm going to sort you a quick bite to eat and then we're going.'

Mary dropped the Sister off in Whitby that night with five minutes to spare before Compline.

The pair had got on so well that Mary returned to Whitby to collect Sister Mary Aldred the following week and drive her to Middlesbrough station to catch the train home.

'If you want prayers for anybody, send me their name and the brief outline,' Sister Mary Aldred offered. 'We pray in Burnham Abbey round the clock – that's our life for Christ. It's a continual prayer: we never stop, with different sisters all involved – one takes over from the other one and we pray throughout the day and night.'

The two stayed in touch but it was only later, by chance, that Mary realised that her friend was in fact the senior Sister at the Abbey. She had happened to mention her name when one of other sisters said: 'You mean Mother Prioress?'

'No. I mean Sister Mary Aldred,' Mary insisted.

'But she *is* Mother Prioress!'

Mary had had no idea, but she smiled for it was confirmation of another valuable lesson – you should always treat people well, if only because you never know who they might be or where you might bump into them again. She also learned that there was always more than one way of seeing something, and, if you truly looked for the goodness, most times you would find it. For those rare occasions when you couldn't, you'd be sure to live a happier life for trying.

From what had seemed like another dark spot in her life, there suddenly appeared much to be thankful for. It was hard to comprehend really, and, for Mary, it just proved how useless worry really was, because with all the worrying in the world she could not have come up with the solutions to her problems that were emerging.

She began telling this story to Reg, but perhaps the story lost something in translation, because he seemed keener to get back to doing whatever work he'd being doing in the garage than hearing about how she'd saved Sister Mary Aldred!

How she'd got it wrong again. Mary returned from taking her vows late on Sunday, and, first thing on Monday morning, Reg was at the door. 'Come into the garage, I've got something to show you,' he said.

Mary went into the garage as little as possible; there was so much stuff in there that just looking at it was enough to start cluttering her mind. Reluctantly, she followed him. In the middle of the garage was something hidden under a dust sheet. Reg stood proudly and pulled it away quickly, as if he was a magician about to unveil his latest trick. The mix of sawdust and dirt in the air caught Mary's breath, and she started to cough. Then she looked, and the sight took her breath for a second time.

'I can hardly believe my eyes! It's so beautiful,' she gasped.

Reg had stripped down two pews, which Mary's daughter, Carol, had salvaged from an old church which was to be demolished, and created a beautiful new one. Mary ran her hand along the smooth wood, polished by her friend's loving hands.

'I made it for you, Mary,' he said. 'Because you were going to the Abbey to make your vows this past weekend, I wanted to get it finished for you coming back. Look, I've carved a cross and dove of peace on the back to make it more personal.'

Reg had noticed that these were the symbols of Mary's new order, and had carved them beautifully into the wood. How could she miss them? Mary was overwhelmed. She had thought he'd taken little notice of what she was doing in Whitby, when all the time he was desperately trying to finish this wonderful gift to help her celebrate it.

26

A SCOTTISH HAVEN

There are some things in life that are better than your wildest dreams, and, for Mary, the place Kath had found for her in Scotland was one of them.

'You didn't tell me it was Keiss Castle!' she said, as they pulled up onto the huge gravel driveway.

'Well, you didn't give me a chance to tell you much about it at all,' Kath replied jovially, and Mary knew that was true. She had been so full of busy when Kath had told her about it that she just trusted her friend would have chosen somewhere suitable.

'Besides, it's not the castle. It's the gatehouse,' Kath added.

'The gatehouse, the castle – it's all the same to me! It's amazing, Kath. Thank you!'

The cottage, as Mary soon came to call it, had two bedrooms, a sitting room with an open fire and a good sized kitchen. There was some work to be done, but Mary was determined to get some shape into it. It didn't take too long to make the place cosy. Mary hired a van to deliver some of her furniture from Teesside, and, once that was in, a burning fire and a boiling kettle were all that was needed for the cottage to feel like home.

While the cottage had been empty, the garden had become overgrown and unwieldy. To tidy it quickly, Mary cleared it all and laid new turf. She then bought a garden seat from an auction, so that she could sit outside and look across the bay. It was like a dream come true. Everything about living there made her feel healthier, and, with new-found energy, Mary bought a second-hand bicycle to get around.

It was while she was cycling around one day that she stumbled upon an old Baptist church. She tried the door, but it was locked.

Every time Mary cycled by it was still locked, so, after a while, she realised it was permanently closed. Looking more carefully, she could see that it had started to rot with neglect. It was situated on the coastline, the same as her cottage, and Mary felt that it was such a shame that it was not being used.

Much to Mary's surprise, the money from her mother allowed her to rent the cottage for three years. When she wasn't there, she lent the key to relatives, friends and many a reverend who wanted a quiet holiday away from a ringing phone. Kath would arrange for the local coal man to drop off eight or ten bags of coal at the cottage, light a fire and warm the beds with hot water bottles ready for the guests. It was always such a delight for Mary to share the joy she received from the cottage. It was also one of the reasons why she couldn't get the ruined old church out of her head.

After some digging, Mary learned that the building had been the first Baptist church in Scotland, and she was appalled that it had been allowed to get into the state it was in. Oh, what she would do with it had she the money. If there wasn't the community in place for it to function fully as a church, she would turn it into a retreat centre so that people could spend however long they needed there, walk on the open moorland, look out onto the sea, breathe in the crisp, clear air and feel healed, just as she had.

She decided to share her idea with the pastor of the nearby Baptist church in Wick.

'I agree with you,' he told her. 'When I first came here, I wanted to do something about that church, if only because of its history.'

'Yes,' Mary agreed. 'I just think it's such a beautiful view that people would want to go there. It's a shame that it's not being used, even if it was only to make it a heritage place or something.'

'Sadly it's really beyond that, in my opinion,' he said.

'How can that be? Surely there must be lottery grants, or some way of raising money to get started?' Mary said, passionately.

He shook his head. 'I've been inside and it's been left for so long that the floorboards are rotten. It's way past simply re-opening it now. I understand how you feel though. I was quite broken too when I found out that nothing was being done about it, but it doesn't belong to the Church any more.'

'Well, who does it belong to then? It must belong to someone.'

'Because it's been out of use so long, it's reverted back to the owners of Keiss Castle.'

Mary's heart sank. The owner of Keiss Castle was an American; she knew that much because the housekeeper had told her one day. However, she didn't know who he was, or if, when living thousands of miles away, he would be interested in restoring a small church on his land.

Sensing her mood, the pastor added gently: 'Don't lose heart about this, because when one person thinks about something, very often someone else does too. You never know what's going to happen.'

Like so many things in life, Mary knew that the fate of that church wasn't hers to control. She'd done what she could for now. Of course, she would continue to pray about it, but there were other issues which needed her immediate attention. Very soon she would return to Teesside, to the day care centre.

27

THE LITTLE THINGS

Mary looked in the mirror and chuckled to herself as she clipped her hair to one side, ready for the glamorous evening ahead. Who would've thought it? Mary Butterwick – Citizen of the Year! She certainly hadn't. Indeed, when the polite young gentleman called to tell her the news, her first response was one of surprise and disbelief.

'What are you talking about?' she asked, bluntly.

'Well, you're the First Citizen of Stockton,' the young reporter replied, taken aback that she hadn't heard of the newspaper's campaign, let alone believed she was the winner. It was the first time that the *Evening Gazette* had presented such an award, and for weeks it had been appealing for nominations from the Teesside public.

Mary hadn't found much time for reading newspapers of late, unless someone else pointed out a story, like when the headline read 'Disappointment for Widow', after planning permission had been turned down to extend 10 Hartburn Lane. It wasn't the best way to find out, but Mary decided that whatever way she learned about the news it wasn't going to change the situation, so there was no point in worrying about it.

Now she was simply stunned. 'Come off it,' she half-laughed, still not quite believing it. 'What on earth are you saying?'

'You've won this award, Mary,' he said excitedly. 'You came above everybody.'

Mary couldn't help warm to his enthusiasm and laughed: 'But for what?'

'For what you're doing, for your work at the day care centre – people are really getting to know about what you're doing now.'

'Well, glory be and alleluia!' she smiled.

Mary knew it was a wonderful honour, but felt slightly embarrassed at the idea of accepting it. The day care centre wasn't just about her. She could never have got this far on her own, even if sometimes it had felt like a lone battle. Still, perhaps she could turn the award into more good; indeed, it was a tremendous opportunity to get the message out about what the Butterwick Trust was trying to achieve.

Just as Mary had imagined, the presentation dinner was a grand affair held at the Swallow Hotel. The editor of the *Evening Gazette* presented her with a trophy cup and the Rotarians gave her a £250 cheque and a souvenir plaque. It was a bit of a palaver, but the £250 was well worth all the ceremony – it was a lot of money, and would start the appeal for beds off nicely.

Accepting the award, she thanked the newspaper, the Rotarians and, not forgetting, the community who voted for her. Then, not one to waste an opportunity, she added: 'I need your support and I will need your support for a long time, because the next stage of the work is beds. If we are going to provide the best possible care for people in their greatest time of need, then we need beds to be able to do that.'

Soon after, the estate agent gave Mary the news she'd been longing to hear. An old convent at 96 Bishopton Road was going up for auction. It was an ideal size and location for what she needed to start the hospice. The church was asking for offers of over £80,000. She put it to the Trustees, who all agreed it was a real find. However, without a fixed price, none of them was able to come up with a proposed offer.

'I don't know,' Mary sighed. 'You're all professional people – bankers and lawyers sat around this table – and you're asking *me* what we should pay for it?'

Mary took the silence to be a 'Yes'! 'Okay, well, there's nothing to do but pray about it and hopefully God will give me a figure,' she declared, without a hint of irony. Her faith hadn't failed her yet, and, if it didn't work out, she trusted that there would be something better around the corner.

A couple of weeks passed, and Mary knew she would have to make a decision. The estate agent told her: 'People are putting in bids. You've got to put yours in now, Mary, otherwise it will be too late.'

'Can't you give me some bearing on the price?' she asked.

'No. All I can tell you is that it must be over £80,000.'

'Can I give it to you this week?'

'Yes, but if you're definitely interested you can't wait much longer, because you're the only one to have looked around and not put a bid in yet.'

So, the pressure was on. Mary prayed and slept on it again. She took her price to the Trustees and it was agreed that a bid should be placed for £90,000. She thought that was a fair price, although she had no idea how they would get the money to pay for it. That was something to think about if the time came.

'It's yours,' the estate agent told her, smiling. 'And they must've really wanted you to have that house, Mary, because we've had offers over £100,000!'

Delighted, Mary took the chairman, Albert, to have another look. Mary asked him to pull up on the side street near the convent. After they'd accepted what had turned out to be such a low offer, she didn't want the nuns to see them pulling up in an E-type Jaguar! Not that she thought it was much to be impressed by. Albert loved it, of course, but she could never understand why anyone would pay so much money to be squashed up like a sardine.

Once inside, neither of them spoke much. They were looking around every room to gauge how much work might be needed to alter the property for their purposes, but Mary didn't want the nuns to think that she would be changing their beautiful convent beyond recognition, and so was keen not to talk about it in those terms openly. The nun showing her around must have recognised Mary's reticence, because she asked if they would like to spend some time looking around on their own. 'You're all right. We know exactly what you're doing,' she added, with a knowing smile.

Mary looked taken aback. What did she mean, 'what she was doing'?

Noticing her reaction, the nun added quickly: 'We know you're working with the terminally ill and that's good enough for us.'

It was going to cost somewhere in the region of £250,000 to buy the convent and do the renovations required to get it up and running as a hospice. There were funds in the bank, but they wouldn't even cover half the cost of the building. Luckily, the nuns were patient. No one was rushing Mary for the money and the nuns never questioned that she would find it.

Unfortunately that wasn't the case with everyone, but Mary soon learned that there would always be naysayers. If she allowed herself to listen to them, she'd never get anywhere. Walking down Stockton High Street, she'd often hear: 'You'll never do that, you know. Where do you think you're going to get £250,000 from?'

To which Mary would reply: 'I don't know, but it'll come. If every house gives me £1, which is much less than the cost of a packet of cigarettes, then we'll have that convent and we'll have it up and running.'

Of course, she knew it wasn't as easy as that, but ignoring the jeers would almost seem like a form of acceptance, as if she was absorbing them in some way. She had to knock them back because cynicism wasn't truth. Of course, raising that kind of money would take hard work. It required a lot of people and a strong backbone, but that's what she and a lot of the community had. Every project, however big, had to start somewhere, and if it was right it would succeed.

As the months passed, the church began to disperse the community who had been living at the convent, until there was only Sister Marie left. She called Mary to ask if she would move in.

'No sister, I can't do that,' she said.

'Of course you can.'

'It wouldn't be right. We haven't got the money for this building yet.'

Mary sensed Sister Marie's disappointment. After living in a community all of her life, at 80 she had suddenly found herself alone. She still occupied the same small room, but, without the community, the convent became an unfamiliar, rambling space around her.

Mary wavered. She too would like some company at the end of the day, somewhere peaceful to go rather than simply retiring upstairs to what was to all intents and purposes a bedsit. The compromise was that Sister Marie would ask her superior, Sister Katherine, and she would ask her Trustees. If they both agreed, then that would provide the answer and she would move in.

Mary lived in the convent for eighteen months before she raised anything like the money to pay the £90,000 agreed price for the building. Both women were delighted with the new set up. Living there was a taste of luxury for Mary compared to Hartburn Lane. Sister Marie had given Mary what had been the bishop's bedroom when he came to visit. Of course, she didn't tell her that, she didn't have to. Mary knew because it was by far the biggest. It had its own bathroom and was next to the chapel. Mary had everything she could possibly need – it was perfect.

In moving there, she'd also found a great friend in Sister Marie and the kind of care she'd not often known, even as a child. Having emphysema meant that Mary rarely got what was known as the common cold. Whenever she caught a chill, it went straight to her chest. Still, no matter how ill she felt, she rarely told anyone. She'd simply get antibiotics from the doctor and take to her bed until the infection cleared. But now she was no longer living alone, it was harder to disguise such setbacks, and she appreciated the care Sister Marie provided. Simply bringing a mug of tea and a piece of toast to her bedside was like a slice of heaven.

In the main, however, when Mary was well, the two of them would share breakfast before Mary left for Hartburn Lane, often not returning until midnight. She would sneak in the front door and tip-toe up the stairs so as not to disturb her housemate. Yet, no matter how late she returned home or how quiet she tried to be, sometimes even crawling up the stairs on her hands and knees, by the time she reached the landing she'd hear Sister Marie's gentle voice: 'Goodnight then, Mary,' to which she'd reply: 'Goodnight, Sister, sleep well,' before making her way down the long corridor to bed.

As winter approached, Sister Marie was allocated a place in a convent in Blackhill, near Consett in County Durham. Mary knew that it would be important for her friend to be in a community for Christmas, but she still didn't have the funds to pay the full price for the convent, and she knew that the nearer it got to Christmas, the greater the possibility that the weather would prevent Sister Marie from travelling north. She remembered John recalling the snow in that area: 'You should see it, Mary,' he'd tell her. She never did, of course. When the weather was like that it was best to stay indoors. If John had trouble digging himself out, then little old Sister Marie stood no chance.

She rang Sister Katherine: 'I'm really getting concerned about Sister Marie – is there any way you could let me pay part of the cost of the building and trust me for the rest of the money so that Sister Marie can go?'

'You are absolutely right,' she agreed immediately, much to Mary's surprise. 'We will trust you for the rest. Sister Marie can go.'

'Thank you, Sister, because I'm concerned in case she's not able to go where she's going.'

However, Mary had no idea how fast things could move once decisions had been made. Within two days of making this arrangement, she received a phone call at work from Sister Marie.

'I'm just ringing to say that the priest is on his way for me,' she said.

'What?' The reality of Sister Marie going finally hit her, and she couldn't stop the words coming out of her mouth. 'They can't do that!'

'I've got to go, Mary. Sister Katherine has released me,' she said calmly.

'Okay,' Mary had to stop feeling sorry for herself and think quick. 'Stop right where you are – I'm on my way. You're not leaving that convent unless I've seen you!'

Mary quickly finished what she was doing, made her excuses and jumped into the car. By the time she got to the convent, the priest had already arrived.

'By gum – you haven't wasted any time,' she told him, her heart racing. She looked at Sister Marie, standing there holding a little case containing all her worldly belongings, and was filled with emotion. She knew it was the right thing. Sister Marie was in poor health. She was partially sighted and had cancer, and needed a good, loving community around her. Mary couldn't provide that – she was out most of the day, which meant that most of the day Sister Marie was alone. She had known that when she had called Sister Katherine to ask for her to be taken to Consett early. Now, however, when it came to her actually going, Mary's heart was not as rational.

'I'm mortified at the thought of you going,' she admitted.

'I know, Mary, so am I,' Sister Marie smiled.

'I'm going to give you a big hug, and then I'm going to have to go first because I can't see you walk away from this building,' she told her, fighting tears. Mary embraced Sister Marie and tried to keep her emotion in. 'Okay. I'm going before you, do you hear?'

Mary shook the priest by the hand; he hadn't deserved her sharpness, but she saw in his face that he understood why. 'You'd better take care of her,' she told him. Turning to walk to her car, she didn't look back. That was how she'd always been and she wasn't going to start changing now.

Back at Hartburn Lane, there was so much to do that Mary got lost in her work, forgetting that she would be returning to an empty house that night. She put the key in the lock and turned it gently to let herself in, the same as she always did. She began making her way softly up the stairs, but, when she got to the last step, there was no tiny voice wishing her goodnight. She shook her head. 'What am I creeping about for? She's not here.'

Mary sat and looked down the stairs towards the door; she could hold the tears back no longer. She buried her head in her hands and sobbed. After five minutes, she wiped her eyes. 'Come on, Mary,' she told herself. 'It's for the best – you know that. Stop feeling sorry for yourself.'

Looking up, she noticed a small light bulb shining in the hallway. She hadn't turned it on when she came in, and she'd been too pre-occupied to turn it off. Mary realised that Sister Marie must have left it on for her, as she always did at night. Even though it was light when she left the convent, Sister Marie had turned on the light knowing that Mary would be returning in the dark.

'She cared for me right until her last time walking out of this convent,' thought Mary. 'After all these years living here, she hadn't thought of herself as she left, she had thought of me.' This time, Mary didn't even try to hold in her tears. 'It's not often people touch your heart in such a way,' she thought. It was the little things that got to her every time.

28

A NEW HOME

Mary woke with a start. What was that noise? It sounded like banging, but surely it was too early for the builders? She looked at the clock: six o'clock in the morning; she'd been in bed just three hours. It had been a long night. The previous night, she had been called by a man whose wife was a day care patient. The woman was dying, it was clear, and Mary had sat with her and her husband until she breathed her last at two-thirty.

Perhaps she'd dreamt the noise? Since the building work had started on the convent there always seemed to be banging. She'd slept in every room in the house, moving around as the work progressed to try to avoid them, but the builders never started this early in the morning.

There it was again. Mary staggered out of bed and made her way to the landing. The knocking got louder. It was the back door. Who could it be at this time? It wasn't yet light. She rushed back into the bedroom, pulled on her dressing gown and ran down the stairs. Then, just as she was about to walk into the kitchen to open the door, she realised who it was.

How could she have forgotten? Sister Marie and the other sisters in the convent always used to give food and drink to the homeless and alcoholics. Now they'd gone, but the men still wanted their sustenance. It wasn't often that Mary felt anxious, but common sense kicked in, and she began to question what she was doing living in such a big building on her own. Now the building work had started, it wasn't very secure. Indeed, the door was only propped shut by a couple of dining room chairs; she only hoped they didn't try to force it.

'It's all right, Sister Marie, don't you get up! I'll see to them,' she shouted to the empty house, before turning to the door adding: 'Okay, okay, I can hear you. You don't have to wake the whole house!'

Mary looked out of the window. There were three of them. She put the kettle on to boil and, opening the fridge, let out a sigh of relief. Luckily there was enough supplies to give her visitors the bacon sandwiches they'd come to expect from Sister Marie. Mary heaped six teaspoons of sugar into each mug, opened the window and handed over the steaming tea. 'Bacon butties are coming,' she chirped. They seemed happy.

There was no point in going back to bed, not now she'd woken up. Making her way upstairs to get dressed, she stopped, noticing the state of the anorak she'd left hanging at the bottom of the stairs. It had been there less than four hours and already it was covered in thick black dust. The builders had warned her that the work would be messy and, with her chest condition, that maybe she should think of moving out while they worked. She now agreed.

Mary had put her name on the council housing list some time ago, and had written several letters to housing associations, but had heard nothing. Perhaps it was time to be more proactive.

She went to the town hall: 'Hello. Can I speak to somebody about accommodation, please?'

'Yes – go and stand over there,' the man behind the desk told her, without lifting his head.

Then, as she was waiting, a woman walked past, stopped and then turned back. 'Aren't you Mary Butterwick?'

'Yes. Why?'

'Well, you don't know me, but you know my husband – he's always talking about you! What are you here for?'

'I'm looking for accommodation – I need somewhere to live.'

'Stop right where you are!'

'I'm not going anywhere,' Mary laughed.

Five minutes later, the woman returned with a handful of keys. 'We'll get the addresses and go and have a look at them. I'm breaking all the rules, but if I don't my husband will kill me.'

It turned out that the woman's husband had a close friend who visited the centre and had dropped him off a couple of times. As the number of lives touched by her dream began to grow, Mary found it difficult to keep track of everyone. Sometimes names and faces became a blur, but she always appreciated the generosity expressed. She was always pleased to meet someone who was enthusiastic about what she was trying to achieve, and the pair chatted animatedly as the woman showed her around some potential new homes.

After the initial viewings, Mary asked if she could revisit a couple of the properties with her son, Keith, later that day. The first, a flat in Norton, had been lived in recently by a young man who had depression, and the colour scheme seemed to reflect his condition. The sitting room had dark brown walls, the bedroom ceiling and walls were navy blue and the bathroom painted in a colour Mary could only describe as sickly green. 'You can't stop here,' Keith declared within seconds of walking in. 'You've never been used to living in a place like this, and you're not starting now! I'm telling you, let's go.'

'What was I thinking, bringing him to this one?' thought Mary. 'It *is* pretty shocking and he's right, there's no way I could live here.' None of the other flats were much better.

Mary took the keys back. 'I'm sorry,' she said, 'But they are all terrible.'

'Wait, we've got another one which has just become vacant in Elm Tree,' said the woman from the town hall. 'Do you want to look at this?'

Mary took the keys and went to see. It was clear that this flat had all been newly decorated. 'This is spot on,' she thought. 'Yes – this is really nice. If I get a bit of second hand carpet in here it will certainly be liveable. This is going to be it. It'll need a bit of oil on that lock though, it's really stiff.' She fiddled with the key on the way out. It had been a little difficult to open as well; she'd have to remember to ask Keith to have a look at that for her.

A woman rushed passed her on the stairs, then, hesitating, turned and asked: 'Do you mind me asking you something?' Then, before Mary could answer, she asked: 'Are you taking this flat?'

'Very possibly,' Mary answered, 'Why?'

The woman went to speak and then paused before replying, in a non-committal fashion: 'Oh, no matter.'

She went to walk away but Mary grabbed her arm: 'What? I don't mean to be rude, but would you mind finishing off what you were going to say?'

'There was nothing, really.'

'Yes, there was, and you stopped yourself telling me.'

'Well, really, I should not say,' she started to bluff her way out of it, but by now Mary was concerned.

'Please, is there something about this flat? Are there some problems around here?'

'Well,' she sighed. 'If you must know, lads come and hang about outside this door. It is trouble on a night.'

'I had noticed the bell had been removed from the front door. Is this the favourite for "knocky nine-doors"?'

'Yeah, they ring the bell all right, but they do more than that on a night. It's probably best you know before you move in.'

Mary took the keys back. Now what was she going to do?

That night, she dreamed about the flat in Norton, but it wasn't navy and brown. The walls were white, cream and pale green – it looked beautiful.

'It's just paint, and I can soon cover up those colours,' Mary thought, on waking. Keith was right, the flat wasn't what she was used to, but nothing in the past few years had been what she was used to. She felt like a sock being turned inside out. Who knew which way was the right one any more?

It turned out to be a good move, and Mary lived happily in the Norton flat for many years, only leaving when the doctor advised her that she shouldn't be climbing stairs. The move also gave her time to concentrate fully on getting the renovations at the convent finished. Of course, there were people who didn't want to move the day care out of 10 Hartburn Lane, but Mary knew the moans and groans, in most cases, were simply expressing the pain of change. Without pain there's no growth, she told herself, while trying to reassure others that the move was something to be celebrating; that it would be better for everyone.

Mary had vested a lot of energy into 10 Hartburn Lane, and it wouldn't be easy for her to say goodbye to it either. She never expressed this, of course. If she wasn't sure of the expansion, how could she expect others to believe it would work? But when the time came there was little room for sentiment. It was late October and the cold dark nights made everything seem longer, still Mary was determined to keep people enthused. 'These people haven't the time to waste in their lives, so we have no time to waste in re-opening either,' she declared.

The Butterwick Trust closed its day care centre at 10 Hartburn Lane after the last patient left on a Thursday, and re-opened in the former convent at 96 Bishopton Road the following Monday.

29

CHANGING HEARTS

Almost a year after moving the day care to Bishopton Road, Mary's dream of opening beds had not materialised. Turning off the lights to lock up after the last of the patients had left, Mary sighed. 'I'm getting tired of passing these bedrooms with no one in them – it's soul destroying.'

She desperately wanted beds, and knew that the need in the community was equally desperate, but at the moment the Trust could not afford it, not without putting the rest of its work at risk. Once the beds were opened, they would need round the clock nursing staff and that wouldn't come cheap. However, knowing that didn't make her frustration any less. It had been exacerbated in recent weeks by the death of her good friend, Nora. During her last days, Mary had visited her twice a day and arranged for district nurses to provide some home care, but she still felt aggrieved that there was no hospice nearby; that there was no bed at Bishopton Road for Nora.

It felt like starting 10 Hartburn Lane all over again, and Mary thought that if she was to get the funds she needed to pull this off, she'd have to first prove something. She didn't yet know what, but something that would enable her to stand up in the community and say: 'I have done this, so can you help me with the rest?'

She called the engineering company where Nora had worked for many years, Davy McKee, and left a message. The following day she received a message in reply, saying that the personnel manager was coming to visit her.

'But she doesn't even know me,' Mary said, astonished.

'She does,' the manager's secretary told her. 'She's heard about you and she wants to come and see you.'

Within a fortnight, the Trust's funds had grown by £12,000 – £6,000 donated from Nora's work colleagues, which the company matched with another £6,000. Mary was elated, but a few days later the urgent needs for beds hit her again when she took two calls from people desperate for care, one of whom was a mother asking for help for her daughter. 'Isn't the pain of losing a child enough without having to fight for basic care?' Mary thought. Inside, she was distraught because, as much as she wanted to help, all she could say was: 'No, I'm sorry. We haven't got a bed.'

That week at church, Stephen surprised her by telling the congregation: 'Today, instead of my usual sermon, we've got Mary Butterwick from the hospice, who is going to tell you what she needs and what the Butterwick Hospice needs.'

Mary could feel her face burning scarlet from embarrassment. But she stood up and started to walk up the altar steps.

'No – go into the pulpit and speak from there,' Stephen told her.

Mary felt she had no alternative, but once she started speaking, the passion she felt for the hospice overtook her nerves and she felt pleased that the vicar had given her the focus she needed.

The next day, her phone rang. 'I believe you are looking for nurses, Mrs Butterwick,' said a man she didn't know.

'Yes, I'm desperately looking for them. Or, at least, the money to pay them,' she replied.

'Well, there's £25,000 on the way to you, so that'll probably pay for two,' he declared.

Mary was speechless, and paused before asking, tentatively: 'Am I imagining this? This is far too serious a matter for you to be having me on.'

'I'm not joking with you, Mrs Butterwick. A cheque is on its way to you today.'

Within a couple of weeks of speaking in the church, Mary had the money to fund five nurses and, to top it all, the cheque eventually came through from the sale of 10 Hartburn Lane.

Mary couldn't arrange a meeting with the Trustees quick enough. Top of the agenda was opening the beds.

'We can't have all this money in the bank and the promise of all these other nurses and not do anything with it,' she told them.

That night it was agreed; the next stage was working out how best to do it. Did they open three beds for a year, or six for six months?

They had to make sure that whatever they decided would work. Mary didn't want to give something to the community only to have it taken away again. At the same time, she was also aware that you couldn't plan for everything, no matter how hard you tried, there would always be obstacles you'd not accounted for. When she had first viewed the convent, her dream was for ten beds. The plans had been passed and she was just waiting for the end of the holiday period to get the building work started, when an official walked in and withdrew the permission.

'You can't have beds upstairs for terminally ill patients,' he had told her.

'Who says we can't?' she asked defiantly.

'I'm saying you can't.'

After examining his credentials, Mary was incensed. 'But your predecessor knew all of this and he gave us planning permission. Go and look and you'll see!'

'Well, I'm the planning officer now, and I'm saying you're not doing it. That's that.'

'Have you ever been into a hospice, Mr Baker?' she asked.

'No, but I don't see what that's got to do with anything.'

'Because then you'd know what you were talking about. We're only talking about having patients up one flight of stairs. How many of your nursing homes have got patients staying two and three floors up?'

He was dispassionate though, and Mary could see she could not touch him. He was a new guy in the post, trying to lay his rules down, and 'jobsworth' didn't even begin to describe his attitude. Nevertheless, she didn't want him to think she was ready to accept his decision just like that.

'Well, whatever is needed to meet your requirements can easily be done,' she had added. 'We can have the equipment to get them down a flight of stairs as easy as a wink if the worst came to the worst.'

But there was no point in thinking about obstacles from the past now – it was really happening. Mary had been given the go-ahead from the Trustees to open three beds, with enough money in the bank to guarantee care for a year. Even before they were ready, Mary had calls from doctors at the hospital wanting to know when they were opening the beds. She couldn't help but smile to herself. Some of these doctors were the same ones who, in the past, would deliberately walk the other way when they saw her, ones who doubted the need for the kind of care she had been campaigning to provide for so long. 'It's happening, Lord,' she prayed gratefully. 'Hearts are changing.'

30

WHO IS MY NEIGHBOUR?

Once opened, the three beds were never empty. At times it frustrated Mary to not to be able to open more, but regulations were regulations and she had to keep up the funds to make sure that the three beds they had could continue once the initial year was up. There were some times in life, however, when she believed you had to bend the rules and hope that no one found out.

Now was one of those times. The hospice only had authorisation to run three beds, but there were six beds on site. Jim was going to die within a matter of days, she felt certain of it. The nursing staff thought so too. None of them was happy to see him go back to the homeless shelter where he'd been sleeping. Of course, it had been a lifeline for him; without the shelter, he would never have come to Butterwick day care. But Mary had been there, and knew it was the last place for the desperate. It was no place to die.

The warden at the shelter would call Mary whenever he found out that one of the men staying there had cancer. Mary would answer: 'Don't worry. I'll be there as soon I as can possibly get. It won't be today but it might be tomorrow.'

Mary would talk to the men, listen to their concerns and fears about the illness and sometimes even accompany them to the hospital. For several months, she had been collecting Jim from the shelter, taking him to the hospital for chemotherapy, bringing him with her to the day care and then taking him back to the shelter at night. She had even scolded the warden.

'Dear me, we can't have this. This is absolutely ridiculous,' she had said upon entering his office.

'What are you talking about, Mary?'

'Well, I've just put Jim to bed and noticed all the burn holes in the bed and in his pyjamas. Dear me, he's laid there smoking as well as being an alcoholic. But it's not just about him – there are another 30 men in there.'

The warden didn't say anything, so Mary continued. 'Are you allowing these men to smoke in a room when they're stoned out of their minds?'

'Well how can I stop them?' he asked, wearily.

'I don't know, but you're going to have to do something drastic, because there is no way I can bring this man backwards and forwards to this when he's terminally ill. He's going to set fire to this place one of these nights, and I can't live with that.'

Mary didn't have to, because the next day, after the day care closed, instead of taking him back to the shelter, Mary and one of the nurses helped Jim onto the stair lift and settled him in one of the empty beds. The nurses would have to do extra night shifts to accommodate him, but they were agreed that he couldn't go back to the shelter in his condition.

Everyone expected him to die within a couple of days, but, a week later, Jim was still with them. None of the staff could understand how he was managing to hold on to life, until he showed them a photograph. It was of his daughter. He told how she'd just had a baby and he was waiting to see her and his new grandchild. No one was sure whether to believe him – there had been no sign or mention of a daughter for all the months Mary had driven him to the hospital.

When the second week past, the question of how to find the extra care began to become more pressing, but no one wanted to let Jim go. During the third week, a woman arrived with a baby to see him. She'd travelled from Brighton and it was early evening by the time she arrived. Mary knew immediately that this must be his daughter. 'I'm so glad you've come,' she said. 'He's been waiting to see you. He'll be thrilled!'

The next day, Jim's conditioned worsened. The staff couldn't hide their tears at realising they were finally losing him, but he told them: 'I don't know why you're all so miserable about me dying. I've had the happiest time of my life since she brought me in here.' He died later that day, and Mary called the warden at the shelter to let him know. No one, other than those who had loved and cared for Jim in his last days, knew officially that he had died at the hospice.

31

THE OTHER SIDE OF
THE WORLD

There had been many blessings at the hospice, but Mary was beginning to think that the time for her to stand aside was approaching. Since opening, the hospice had filled a need that never lessened, so there was still plenty of work to be done. Nevertheless, Mary began to think was that her own work there was done.

'Perhaps it's time I walk away and retire,' she thought. Of course, there was always something for her to do, but she was sure that, if she left, the hospice would go on running just as well on its own. Maybe it was time that she stepped down, or perhaps it was just time to take a break.

Outside of her short trips to Scotland, it was ten years since Mary had last taken a proper holiday. It was now almost as long since she'd seen her cousin, Peggy, and she missed her so. They still wrote often and spoke on the phone, but now Peggy and Trevor were in Australia it wasn't the same. No matter how clear the voices at the end of the phone, Mary knew they were no longer just a couple of hours away in Southport, and she didn't know when – or even if – she would see them again.

It was no longer true to say that the hospice needed her. She knew full well that its day-to-day running would tick along just fine. If she wanted to see Peggy, which she did, then this was as good a time as any.

Mary's children pooled together to provide the money for her airfare, and there was a further surprise. Shortly after she decided to go, Mary attended a charity night at Middlesbrough Football Club. Over the years, she had gotten used to the format – there would be a dinner, a speaker and perhaps an auction, and any money raised would be donated to the hospice. However, this time was different. Mary arrived to discover that the charity night was also a birthday party for her – and still that wasn't an end to the surprises. When it came to what Mary felt was the best bit of the evening – learning what the revelry had raised – the speaker for the evening, television presenter Martyn Lewis, presented Mary with a donation for the hospice before handing over an additional cheque which was for her.

'I've heard rumours that you've always wanted to go to Australia to see your relatives, so now you can,' he said.

Mary was touched and delighted. She called Peggy to say she was coming, and booked the next flight she could, to return in three months time. 'Australia, here I come!'

Peggy and Trevor were equally delighted to see Mary. It had been far too long for all of them, and there was much to catch up on. However, no sooner had Mary got to Australia, than she collapsed with exhaustion and had to spend the first three weeks of her holiday in bed.

It was only when she stopped that Mary realised just how hard she had been working, and how tired she really was. Now it was her turn to be cared for, and Peggy took on the role easily, with the generosity of heart that Mary so loved her for. Being forced to stay still also gave the cousins all the time they needed to chat and catch up properly on where their lives had taken them in the past decade.

Peggy and Trevor had become active members of a lively Pentecostal church, which was always open to ideas about how more care could be brought into the community. Peggy had been telling them about Mary's work at the hospice, and the congregation was keen to hear more. Mary agreed, and, as soon as she was feeling better, it was arranged for her to speak at the Sunday morning service.

After the service, one of the church leaders asked her: 'Would you consider staying and doing something here like you've done in England – with the church's backing, of course?'

Mary did consider it. After all, she had already considered stepping down from her role at Butterwick hospice. This community had nothing in place like the hospice; they didn't even have organised bereavement counselling. There was much she could do here, and being with Peggy again was wonderful.

Many years earlier, Mary had thought seriously about immigrating to Australia under the 'Ten Pound Pom' scheme of the 1960s. At the time, Keith had just left school and was finding it difficult to find the kind of work he wanted. The Australian government was actively encouraging families to emigrate from the UK with bargain £10 fares. Both Mary and John thought that the opportunities in Australia would be better for the children. However, not all of the family agreed. Mary's mother, who was living with them at the time, was set against uprooting at such a late stage in her life, and Carol, who had fallen head over heels in love with Tony, couldn't bear the thought of moving so far. Mary smiled as she recalled how, despite her own whirlwind young courtship, she had thought Carol much too young to know her own heart. If only she knew then what a good son-in-law Tony would turn out to be.

In the end, John got fed up with the arguments about the idea and threw the official application papers, which had been filled out, into the open fire. Mary was hugely disappointed at the time – the challenge of setting up a new life had seemed so exciting. Now, more than 30 years later, she was being given another chance.

As with all big decisions, Mary didn't agree to anything before she'd prayed about it. Yet, this time, she felt her heart was telling her to say 'No'.

'I'm sorry, I can't stay. It is too big a commitment and I have commitments at home in England,' she told them. However, before she left, she led some training in bereavement counselling and helped to set up some bereavement groups in the area, so that they had the foundations on which to build themselves.

It was hard to leave, but the time away had cleared her mind. She had renewed her relationship with Peggy and Trevor and, at the same time, she had realised that she wasn't ready just yet to step away from the hospice. There was more work she could do there; she had just been too exhausted to see it clearly, never mind start doing it.

As the plane pulled in to land, Mary looked out of the window. Down below, she could see a huge Union Jack and she smiled because, before she left, Val had told her: 'You can't see much from the sky, but you'll always see a Union Jack.' It must be her. As the plane got closer, she saw another banner, with the words *Welcome Home, Mary!* It was her friends, waiting eagerly for her; she was home, and she knew instantly it was where she should be.

32

ON THE MOVE – AGAIN

'It's amazing what a difference a change of scenery can make to your outlook and energy levels,' Mary thought. Since returning from Australia, she'd found renewed enthusiasm for her work, and set up a drop in centre for the bereaved in addition to the day care and the hospice's bedded unit.

The extra services were proving more popular than she could have imagined, and, with numbers growing all the time, it was becoming increasingly difficult to find space for everybody. If the work was going to continue to expand in this way, then the hospice would need more space. Mary still held onto her dream of ten beds. To reach that number, they would need to extend or move, so Mary prepared herself for another period of upheaval, and prayed that the community would support her in it.

It was originally thought that the land to the back of Bishopton Road could be used, but when plans were drawn up for what was needed, it turned out that the space wasn't quite big enough. There was some suitable land next to North Tees Hospital in Stockton, which was available on a leasehold basis. Mary did have some reservations about being so close to the hospital, because she didn't want it to be thought of as one and the same. That was important to her, and it always surprised people who were arguing that the government should fund the hospice when she argued the opposite.

'We do get some funds from the hospital trusts, but if the authorities paid for everything then they would take over, deciding how we should spend the money, and it would just become a mini-hospital,' she reasoned. 'We are *not* a hospital. We are looking after people at the end of their lives, giving the patient and their family time to stop and care, to say what they feel, and show they love each other. This place is all about love. Without the love of the community it can't exist, and I think that's how it should be. It's a psychological thing – you help me, and I help you. People need that – to feel useful and wanted.'

Being next to the hospital wouldn't have been Mary's first choice, but she could see some benefits of the proximity for patients. Also, there were so many rules and regulations that the hospice came under now for its licence, that she recognised its independence wasn't what it was.

She would hold her tongue during an inspection, but it didn't stop her thinking: 'The way they come in here and nit pick over something as small as we can't have a pedal bin! I wish they'd do it in the blasted hospitals, because if they did there wouldn't be half the problems there are today.'

The location aside, there were lots of other positive aspects to the possible move, not least having a purpose-built building and the facility to accommodate ten beds, as she'd always dreamed they would do.

Once the site was agreed, there was still much to do, like raising the £1.2 million to pay for it. As always, there were the doubters. 'Where do you think you'll get £1.2m from, Mary?'

Of course, Mary knew it was a difficult task, but it wasn't going to be made easier by those dismissing it out of hand. Discouragement wasn't anything new. The figures might be higher this time, but the jeers were the same and Mary batted them back now as she did then. 'If everyone in this town gives me £1, then we'll get there – don't you worry.'

Even as she said it, Mary thought: 'It is one thing saying you are going to put out an appeal for so much money, but it's a lot to stick your neck out for.' Sister Mary Aldred's words came back to her: 'Where God goes the Lord must provide, Mary.'

She knew there was no way the hospice had anywhere near £1.2m, but she moved out in faith and prayed it would come. 'I'm going to have to work my butt off again for this one, but knowing that God is going to provide … Well, that makes all the difference in the world,' she told herself.

Mary decided that whatever she could get free was extra money to spend on something else, so she began ringing round to see what firms were willing to donate. There was so much needed for a new building that she hadn't even considered. British Steel provided £10,000 worth of ash, which was needed to prepare the land for building. Next, she went through the *Yellow Pages*, looking for possible donors of iron mesh and plastic lining for the foundations. Those materials that she didn't get for free, she managed to get a good discount on. She even struck a deal on the bricks.

Nevertheless, this was a task she couldn't take on alone. Every day, she would go down to the land and pray for help. She was aware that many who saw her there believed she was crazy, but she'd heard it all before, and, whatever anyone wanted to say, she knew that the hospice wouldn't be there without God's guidance. That said, the hospice wasn't the same as it was when she had founded it. More than a decade on, it was now a sizable organisation, and, with that, came corporate responsibilities towards a secular society. Its politically correct style of management made faith a public irrelevance.

It was another several years before Tony Blair's spokesman Alastair Campbell was to famously interrupt the Prime Minister during an interview with the line: 'We don't do God.' Yet some might say that he was just voicing what many heads of prominent organisations had been thinking for years, lest they say anything which could cause offence.

Mary didn't understand the political sensitivity that had emerged around faith. It seemed all stuff and nonsense to her. Once the foundations for the new building were in place, a celebration was organised. The new plans also included a children's hospice, and Mary was thrilled that the first turf was to be cut by the parents of a young girl who had died of a brain tumour.

She didn't mind keeping a lower profile; the hospice had been built for and by the community of Teesside, and it was only right that others should begin to front it. What saddened her was the thought of not being able to give thanks to God on such a happy day. Most people who came to the hospice knew where she was coming from spiritually, and accepted that as she accepted them. The care offered at the hospice was for everyone – people of all faiths and people of none. It always had been and always would be. As far as she was concerned, God would have us care for each other and no one could move beyond that.

When the day came, before leaving she set aside some quiet time to pray, as she did every morning. She opened her book of daily readings and there it was: her reading for the day was the same chapter and verse – Philippians 4:19 – that she had received from Albert on the night of the house blessing in Hartburn Lane:

My God will fulfil all your needs out of the riches of his glory in Christ Jesus.

For Mary, this was a sign of God reaffirming his place at the centre of her work. Up until then, she had begun to doubt the progress of the purpose-built centre. It was such a challenge, but was it the right one? Now, she felt more than ever that they were on the right track, if only they could hold out in faith.

She picked up the phone and called Albert. 'You're not going to believe this.'

'What? What's happened?'

'Just get your daily reading out, because you'll have a fit when you do. It's the very verse you sent me when I opened Number 10!'

'Is it?'

'Yes – have a look. Now what am I going to do about that?'

'Well, you're going to have to stand up and say it.'

'What?'

'Today at the opening of the launch – stand up and tell them.'

Mary wasn't sure. 'Do you really think I should?'

'Yes.'

Mary put the reading in her bag. When she arrived at the site, there was a big marquee up, and local television personality, Paul Frost, was the *compère*. Everyone said their bit and then Paul passed Mary the microphone.

'I'm saying very little here today, but I believe it's an important thing to say,' she said. Mary then began to recall her experience that morning, and read the relevant reading. In the crowd, she heard a voice say: 'Look at her, Bible punching!' Of course, she knew that the reading was probably meaningless to most of the people there, but it was important to her and she quietly tried to ignore the comments. 'God's hand must be upon us when this kind of thing happens,' she told the crowd. 'That's his way of letting us know we are doing the right thing, or of letting me know anyway.'

Afterwards, she said to Albert: 'I shouldn't have done that. I've really put the cat among the pigeons with this one.'

Part 5

A SEASON
FOR EVERYTHING

33

EXCEEDING EXPECTATIONS

Three years after the first turf was cut, the new, purpose-built Butterwick Hospice opened on 22 July 1997. It had beds for ten inpatients, and day care facilities for 20 patients a day. Work on the children's unit had to be postponed, as the funds had fallen too short to complete everything. To continue building the children's wing would have put the whole project at risk, and, as Mary told those who enquired: 'It's not forgotten, but to carry on now would put the adult hospice at risk, and without the adult hospice there wouldn't be a children's hospice.'

It was a disappointment, but one that couldn't be dwelt on too long. You only had to look at the new building to see how much had been achieved, and to concentrate solely on what was still to do would have seemed ungrateful. It was all that Mary had set out to do and more. Walking in through the double doors to the reception, it felt so spacious, yet the designers had managed to keep all the cosiness and homeliness that Mary had envisaged when she first set out at 10 Hartburn Lane.

So much had changed, yet so much was the same that the move felt like a natural evolution. On the wall by the reception desk was a photo of John, in whose memory the hospice was founded all those years ago. Mary felt his image grew more handsome by the day. 'It's not half bad, this place, is it, John?' she thought. Oh, how she wished he was here to see it, to share it with her. In her heart, he shared it with her. He was in everything she did for the hospice – every thought, action and word.

To the left of the entrance were lots of comfy sofas, and, seeing them, Mary nodded in approval; families needed to be comfortable at times like this. There was a proper canteen too. Well, it was more than a canteen – it was like a mini-restaurant which served good nourishing food for visitors as well as patients, even three-course meals if they so wished. 'Yes, this place was about recognising the simple but good things in life,' Mary thought. 'The little things that we may not always notice, but, if they're taken away, life suddenly becomes so much more uncomfortable.'

Mary walked around the day care. The big, solid wooden tables the nuns had left in Bishopton Road were still there. There was, of course, a lot of new equipment in the wards, and wonderful facilities for bathing and relaxation that they could never have hoped for in the previous locations. Walking into the chapel to give thanks, Mary couldn't help but smile. All around her were memories of the people who had helped her build the hospice into what it had become. Pinned on the walls was work from children at local schools who'd been involved in fundraising; the way the community had supported the hospice, and continued to, was such a blessing.

She moved her hand fondly along the smooth lines of the carving on the pew Reg had spent hours perfecting. Then her eyes were drawn to a beautifully carved picture, including the words of the Lord's prayer, on the wall. So many people had remarked on how lovely it was when they came into the chapel for the first time. You couldn't help but notice it. She smiled, remembering one of the patients, Harold, who had donated it. When he had handed it to her it was so blackened with age that she could hardly make out what it was. It had belonged to his great grandfather, and had been stored away in an attic for years.

Harold had asked Mary if she knew anyone who could clean it up. She couldn't think of anyone, no one who wouldn't cost a small fortune anyway, but she said she'd try. As Reg had done such a marvellous job on restoring and carving the pew, she asked his opinion. He took it away and brought it back as good as new, with only a small black mark left on it. 'I left that there purposely, to make it look authentic and old, because it is,' he told her.

Mary was delighted and had taken it herself to Harold's house. He had lost the movement in one arm after a stroke, so she knew he wouldn't be able to carry it home from the day care himself.

'What do you think?' she beamed.

'That's great!'

'Well, as long as you're pleased with it.'

'I'm delighted,' he smiled.

'So, where would you like me to put it now you've got it back?'

'I'm not putting it anywhere, but I hope you do,' he said.

'What?'

'It was for you anyway. I knew if you were asking to clean it for yourself you wouldn't do it.'

'You rogue,' she laughed.

'Please accept it. We've no call for it here and we'd like to think you had it.' It had been a feature of the hospice ever since.

'Everyone who lived and loved in the hospice left a mark of kindness,' she thought. Yes, many died there and many more would die here. There would be many tears, but there was also much laughter, because everyone who died at the hospice also lived at the hospice and Mary hoped that the care provided allowed them to enjoy their lives and celebrate what was most important in life.

Oh, how she wished she could explain it better sometimes. Or, at least, she wished that more people could come to understand the vision of a hospice as she saw it. So many times, she heard people talk about hospices as if they were simply a place where someone goes to die. It all sounded incredibly morbid. Death was a natural part of life; did we have to keep running from it to the point where the fear stopped us enjoying the life we have?

As she left the chapel, she bumped into a man who'd been over to the hospital to collect some things for a relative.

'We've just been over to the hospital, Mary, and all the nurses are dying of curiosity to know what it's like in here,' he enthused. 'It's a pity they don't come and find out because ever so many stopped me and asked.'

'So what did you tell them?' Mary asked.

'I told them it was like a five-star hotel with a bunch of angels looking after it.'

Mary smiled; perhaps she didn't need to be worrying about explanations any more.

A year later, following the death of Princess Diana, the *Northern Echo* newspaper launched an appeal in her memory to raise £500,000 for Butterwick Hospice, and the children's wing was completed with the money. The hospice was now everything Mary had dreamed of and more.

34

STACKING UP AWARDS

'Who would have ever thought it? Me – a Master of Science,' Mary chuckled to herself. 'I don't know the first thing about science, but I guess they've just thought it is the nearest thing to what I do.'

When Mary accepted her honorary degree at Teesside University, she was given a standing ovation. At first she thought the huge applause was for someone else, until a professor pointed out that it was indeed for her. He later told her: 'I've never seen a standing ovation at a degree ceremony in my life.'

It was a wonderful day and, although Mary didn't know it, there were many more like it to come. The same year, Mary was honoured by Stockton Council with the Freedom of the Borough. In a ceremony at the town hall she was presented with a scroll and a freeman's jewel. They were both special gifts, but what meant most to Mary was the recognition of the hospice by the community, and the ability it gave her to express her heartfelt thanks for the continuous support she'd been given.

'As I stand here today,' she said, 'I have very mixed feelings, both proud and humble, as I reflect back on the past 20 years of my life since my husband John died.

'His death, and its circumstances, not only changed my life – it brought hospice care to Stockton. It changed a way of care in this community and, with it, many people's lives. I felt strongly that there must be a better way of caring for a dying person and their family than I and my family had experienced.

'It was through John's death that I realised many things could and should be different. I felt more and more strongly that something had to be done about it, and so a hospice was born.

'Only very recently, I saw a small news cutting which started by saying: "Mary Butterwick's life has touched thousands of lives." I think I really realised that for the first time when I read that. Because there has always been so much to do, I haven't really reflected on what a difference it has made. But as I read it, it made me feel very humble. All those people have given me so much – they have made my life richer. For the first seven or so years in the hospice, my lot was a very lonely one, but it was all those thousands of people who kept me going. The patients and their care have always been my driving force.

'I am also full of admiration for our doctors, nurses and for all the staff, not forgetting our wonderful team of volunteers. I believe there are none to beat them – they are the best. But we could not do all that we do to care for people whose illness cannot be cured, and their relatives and friends, without the widespread support of the local community. It is not our hospice, it is your hospice. It belongs to the people of this Borough of Stockton and its surrounding community. In this way, you care for me as I care for you. Butterwick Hospice has done a lot for health care in our society, and I am thankful indeed; very thankful to each one who, over the years, has been involved, for their love and support.

'None of this would have taken place without God's help, and what he showed me and brought me through. He gave me the love, strength and determination to persevere and dedicate my life to it.

'I am grateful for the support of many people and particularly the support that my family gave me. Without them nothing would have been achieved in the beginning. So, I would like to take this opportunity of publicly thanking them and for bearing with my single-mindedness. Today, as you honour me, you honour them and everyone associated with the Butterwick Hospice and all those who enter its doors.

'On behalf of all of us, I say to the Mayor and members of Stockton Borough Council, "Thank you." '

In the New Year's honours list of 2003, Mary was appointed an Officer of the Order of the British Empire, in recognition of her contribution to the hospice movement nationally. Again, it was a wonderful day, although she joked that you weren't allowed to take your own photographs so you had to fork out a small fortune on the official ones. There were no charity discounts to be arranged for that.

35

SEARCHING FOR A PURPOSE

The question of whether it was time for Mary to step away from the hospice kept coming back, but each time she confronted it something inside – she couldn't always say exactly what – would stop her, and she would stay.

However, it was no secret that she couldn't do as much as she once did. She was getting old too, although she often wondered if those around her noticed. In 2004, aged 80, she decided to step down from her official role in the hospice chaplaincy. Having more time on her hands, she invited her old friend Audrey – from her army days – to Stockton, and drove the pair of them to Scotland to see Kath. Not wanting to put Kath out of her bed, they stayed at a nearby farm house and spent two weeks reminiscing and breathing in the clear, crisp sea air that always made Mary feel fully alive.

'Perhaps now is the time to retire to the coast, to live by the sea and breathe like this every day,' she wondered.

After the break, she returned to the hospice to learn that one of her favourite managers, Andrew, was leaving. He explained that it wasn't anything that he was unhappy with, simply that he felt he'd gone as far as he could with them career-wise, and needed to move on to progress.

'I'm not a dimwit,' Mary told him. 'I have lived, you know, and I do understand from your point of view. But, saying that, I'm very sad to see you go because you are a lovely person and just the type of person we need here.'

'You've taught me so much, and it's going to break me up leaving this place,' he told her. 'I can't thank you enough.'

'But why am I here, Andrew? I'd be grateful if you could tell me, because quite honestly I don't know any more.'

Andrew was confused. 'I don't know what you mean!'

'Well, I sit here and I talk to the patients, of course I do. If a person comes up and a nurse says "Will you talk to these people?", I'll go and do it. Or, if a reverend needs to come in and get familiar with the place, I will phone him up and sort it out. I know, I do all sorts of things. I'm not lacking in something to do in that sense, but it's not a specific role. I don't want to get too involved in the chaplaincy any more, because I don't want to step on the toes of those who are doing it now and doing a good job. What am I doing here? At my age now, don't you think that I should walk away from this place?'

'But you can't,' he said, surprised that she would even think it. 'You of all people, you can't walk away.'

'But tell me why? I'd be glad to know, because why do I sometimes struggle to get up in the morning to come here?'

'You can't because you *are* this place, Mary,' he told her, as honestly as he could. 'When I go out into the community, it's not the Butterwick Hospice people talk about, it's Mary Butterwick. It was because of you that I came here in the first place – because I had heard about you and the work you'd done. You might think you have no role here, but you are seen as representing the hospice. You'll never be able to walk away from this place, Mary, because you *are* the hospice and that's how people see you.'

'Yes, but there's got to be something more than that, Andrew, surely?'

'Yes – you are the presence here.'

Mary was surprised to hear him say it, because that was exactly how she'd felt in the past few years. Sometimes she felt that she didn't need to say or do anything, but that people just behaved in a certain way because she was there. Like the head teacher, so to speak, there would be no misbehaving when she was around; she expected people to treat others well, and to value a caring attitude above all. While she was there, love was to be at the heart of any work done, even if her views did cause the odd squabble among the management.

Mary smiled to herself. She'd never set out to do any of this in that sense. As far as she was concerned, she'd simply set out to fulfil a human need. She believed that the recognition she had received must have stemmed from those early years, when she was the administrator-cum-director. When she was starting off she did so many different jobs because there wasn't the money to pay anyone else to do them. She spoke to everyone who came through the doors, and sat with so many families with breaking hearts. She did that for more than twenty years, so perhaps she shouldn't be surprised to hear that so many people knew her or associated the hospice with her.

Okay, so she had no specific role now, but a job was a job. A Christian never retired in that sense. God's work for us here is never done; there is always someone to care for, someone to help, someone to love. Mary's presence at the hospice was an expression of all of those things. How had she not recognised how that was valued? Perhaps it wasn't time to move on, but to reflect and value that goodness too.

36

REFLECTIONS ON A LIFE

Mary opened her daily reading. It was the Parable of the Sower, Jesus' story of a farmer planting his seeds. Some fell on the road and the birds ate them; some fell on rocks, quickly growing into plants, but because the roots weren't deep enough, they died; other seed fell among weeds, which choked the young plants as they tried to grow. Then there was the seed that fell on good ground, which grew well and produced a harvest, multiplying many times. Jesus later compared the seed that fell on the good ground to a person who hears his teaching and understands it. That person grows and produces fruit – sometimes thirty, sometimes sixty, sometimes a hundred times more.

Mary smiled. It was a passage that had helped her so much in the early days. It showed how God blessed those who trusted in him. So many times, when starting up the hospice, Mary had felt like she was scattering seeds. Now she could see that no seeds planted with the right heart were ever wasted. Those fruits were for everyone to see in the hospice. Who would have guessed how much those first tiny seeds would grow? Not even Mary could have imagined how many people would become involved. The staff and patients of the hospice were only part of the story – now there were people who climbed mountains for them, who trekked through jungles and bungee-jumped off the Transporter Bridge! It was amazing to think about how far they had come.

It was 2009, 25 years since Mary had opened the first day care centre. Now the main site at Stockton provided ten adult beds and four children's beds as well as day care. There was another day care centre at Bishop Auckland, and three more offshoots attached to hospitals in Sedgefield, Stanhope and Barnard Castle. In addition to that, the hospice funded a team of palliative care nurses to go out into homes in the North Tees and South Tees areas.

It cost £3 million a year to keep it all going. She remembered the early jeers: 'Where do you think you'll get £75,000 from, Mary?' She didn't know then, and she still didn't know now how the money came in, but it did. A proportion of the money was from the government, but the majority still came from the community who continued to support the work.

Teesside people had built the hospice, not with taxes, but with their hearts. They wanted it, they valued it and they kept it going. Mary hoped that its core values of love and responsibility would never change. It had certainly been a journey, and one that she couldn't have taken alone. We can feel that we're on our own, but we're not really, she mused.

Looking back, Mary knew that she had been blessed, even when she had been unable to see it. She realised that we can, and do, return to living and enjoying life again after bereavement. John's death had changed her life beyond recognition. Back then he was her life, and, after such a personal loss, it was obvious that the life she was left with was going to be vastly different from the one she knew. She realised in time that, as life becomes different, so you can make it into something good, something special again. That is how we all go on living.

At one point Mary would have liked another relationship, because, despite how others might think of middle-age, she didn't feel old, not too old for romance anyway – she wondered if any of us ever are. Mary still missed John. She missed so many little things personal to him, but she also missed having a male companion, a man to go out with and to come home to. Now that her work with the hospice had slowed down, she felt that ever more acutely. At the same time, Mary knew she had to let that part of her life go, because she couldn't commit her all again. In the early days, she had to give everything to the hospice. It wouldn't have lasted and grown without dedication. Someone had to keep everyone motivated, to fuel the fire to keep it going.

She laughed, remembering. Where had she got all that energy from? 'Someone must have prayed for me a lot when I was younger,' she thought. She guessed it was probably her mother, although she suspected now that her Auntie Edith used to send up a lot of prayers for her too. Perhaps her father did as well. She had never thought of him as a religious man, or even knew he had a faith until after he died and a small card bearing a cross was removed from his pocket. We never really know how many people are praying for us, wishing us well and blessing our lives. Now, whenever Mary was stuck in traffic because of an accident, heard a siren or passed a funeral, she sent up a little prayer: 'God, there is someone in trouble. Please look after them and keep them close to you.'

Mary prayed for her own children every day, although they were far from children any more. No doubt having her as a mother hadn't always been the easiest of rides. For the first 20 years of the hospice, she knew that she was never really there for her children or her grandchildren. Her days, and most of her evenings, were spent building the foundations of what she saw today. At the time, she could not see what her dreams would become, nor visualise the personal cost.

Mary had known that, working the hours she did, time with her family was limited. If any of the children had wanted her to go for a day out, she couldn't. In that way she had missed a lot, but she knew that was how it had to be. Having always been family-oriented, it wasn't something she took lightly, and she prayed about it a lot, asking God for guidance.

Mary reasoned that yes, they were her children, but they were also adults with lives and families of their own. Perhaps she couldn't have a close involvement in that part of their lives, but she knew that she would always be a part of their lives, because she would always be their mother. She believed that as we honour God, so God will honour us. She trusted that in so doing he would let them feel her love in their hearts.

Mary looked at the family photograph on the wall. It always pleased her to see them together and smiling. Oh, if only she could have wrapped each one of her children in a bubble of joy and protected them from any ills of the world then she would've done. There had been hurts and misunderstandings, but she had always tried to do everything with a good heart, and prayed that God would heal any mistakes she'd made along the way.

Mary knew that it didn't do to dwell on paths that weren't taken; we can reflect, but we can't turn back. Life, by its very nature, was complicated and even in her eight decades she still hadn't finished with its lessons. But it was time to stop trying to make neat any loose edges. There would always be things in her life that she wouldn't understand, but in her heart she knew that in every sacrifice she made, God hadn't really deprived her of anything. Those same grandchildren who were little when she set off were now grown-up. Despite missing out on much of their childhood, Mary had good relationships with all of them, sometimes perhaps enhanced by the experiences she could now share.

Karen, the baby John and her had taken the trip to see just a month before he died, was now a teacher in London. After starting work, she was shocked to find so many of the children had parents who were dying or had been diagnosed with a serious illness.

'Nana, what am I going to do for all these kids?' she'd ask.

'Just take it slowly, Karen, and keep your eyes well and truly open,' Mary advised. 'Children don't understand. They can't say to you, "This is because I've just lost my mother", or "I'm afraid". But watch very closely, because their actions will tell you. Get them to draw a picture of how they feel today – you'll be amazed at what comes out.'

Karen enrolled on a bereavement counselling course, but every time she came up against an obstacle she would phone Mary, who would say: 'Okay, if you've got time, sit there and tell me what you feel about this child.'

After a few weeks of this, Karen said: 'The head sent for me today.'

'The headmaster? Why? Have you been doing something good or doing something rotten?'

'Actually the head asked me about my children.'

'What do you mean?'

'Well, he said: "How is it that you seem to know more about children when they've got problems than some of the teachers who've been here for years?" So I said: "That's easy – it's because I've got the best counsellor in the North-east of England helping me: my nan!" '

STILL DREAMING

'It is sometimes harder to sit beside the bed than to be in it,' Mary thought. She knew that sounded strange, but sometimes she believed it was easier to be the patient than to be the family watching a loved one suffer. If there is one certainty in life, it is that all of us will die, and usually when a patient came to the hospice he or she was reconciled to the fact that it probably would be his or her time soon. For everyone else involved, they've not just got to cope with the loss of a loved one, but with facing their own mortality and the uncertainty of when and how death will come.

Mary saw it with staff all the time. It wasn't an easy thing to cope with, and, for some, it was too much. Mary often felt that once you had come to accept death as part of life, then you could enjoy living. She liked to think that life, however short, was still being enjoyed at the hospice. There was certainly plenty of laughter and Mary believed that, most of the time, the place lifted the spirits of everyone there rather than knocking them down. There was so much joy to be found. Indeed, the only thing that really made her angry was when people didn't have the right heart.

Mary believed that walking with someone on their final path was the greatest gift anyone could give. Perhaps it was because she was denied that time with John that she valued it so much. It still hurt that she never told him one last time how much she loved him. She loved and missed him still.

Mary had been watching two brothers. It was the younger of the two, Martin, who was dying, and Stephen was terrified to leave his side.

'You go and get yourself some rest,' she told him.

'But what if ...'

'What if you were to simply turn away and your brother was to go? That's how quick death can come,' she told him.

'I know, but I feel I should be doing more, that I'm not doing enough.'

'All we really need to do is give the person some of the love we have inside of us,' she smiled. 'You are giving Martin the greatest gift by just being here. You're giving of yourself, and that's real love.'

'I'm just not sure I can do it.'

'If you've got the heart to do it, God will give you the strength to do it. And he will for Martin too. As God gives us the grace to live, he'll give us the grace to die when the time comes.'

'We used to go camping together,' he told her. 'Martin wants to go to Spain. If he can go, I'd like to take him.'

It was too late for that, Mary knew, but she also believed that it's never too late to follow a dream; you just have to realise what it is about the dream you are really looking for.

The next day, she asked Martin, in Stephen's company: 'What is it about going to Spain that you want most of all?'

'I want to drink sangria and eat paella. I want to walk along and feel the sun on my face, to see its rays bounce and sparkle on the water. I want to see the sea extend as far as my eyes can see, to hear the waves crash against the shore and smell the salt in the air,' he smiled.

Mary could picture it as he talked. 'It does sound wonderful,' she smiled. 'But most of that you can do off the cliff tops at Whitby.'

The two brothers laughed.

'Well, think about it,' she said, jovially, thinking she could possibly help to arrange a short trip to Whitby – she was sure Martin could manage that. 'Everything you've basically told me there about why you'd like to go to this place in Spain you can do in Whitby. Think about it, we'll see how things go – take it on a daily basis and maybe we can go.'

Martin smiled, genuinely, his eyes twinkling with enthusiasm. 'What's your dream, Mary?' he asked.

'Well, there is this place that has always been close to my heart,' she began, before adding, quickly: 'But it's just a dream. Sometimes you have to lay a dream down, you don't complete it. It always stays a dream.'

'But what is it, Mary?' they both asked, and she could see they wanted to know. She'd started now, so she guessed she might as well share it with them.

'There is a church in Scotland, and it's been left to go derelict. I used to go up there ... Well, I hope to go again one day, but I don't know when it'll be. My good friend, Kath, who I used to visit there, has now passed away.

'This particular church was the first Baptist church ever built in Scotland. Whenever I visited Kath there, I used to know that God used that time to heal my spirit. It's such a wonderful place, so quiet and peaceful, and the scenery is breathtaking. When I sit there and look out to sea, I can be miles away in no time. I know God healed me in my bereavement a lot by taking me up there to that wonderful part of the world.

'Now, if I had something like £1 million, I'd just love to turn that derelict old Baptist church into a place where people could stay, enjoy a retreat, go outside and look out to sea and be transported. After a few days, I'd guarantee that God would've healed them. That's a dream I've had for years.'

A couple of days later, when Mary was back in Martin's room, he said: 'We've got something to tell you today, Mary.'

He looked at his brother and gave a knowing wink. 'Okay, are you sitting comfortably?'

Mary had no idea what the pair were conjuring up between them, but they seemed like naughty school boys again. Martin handed her a white envelope with her name written in big letters across the front.

'What's this?' she asked.

'Something to start your dream – you know, the dream you were telling me about.'

There were several hundred pounds in the envelope. Mary felt she couldn't take that from him.

'What are you doing? You can't give me that! Besides, I told you, I'd need a million at least!'

'I know – but every dream has a beginning and there's your beginning, Mary.'

'Thank you,' Mary said, touched. Here was a dying man, who, despite his pain, could see the beginning of something. Even at the end of his life, he still had the ability to dream. 'If you see Jesus before I do,' she smiled, 'give him my love.'

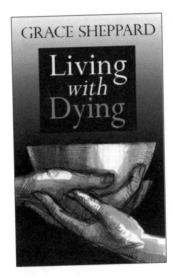